$8⁵⁰

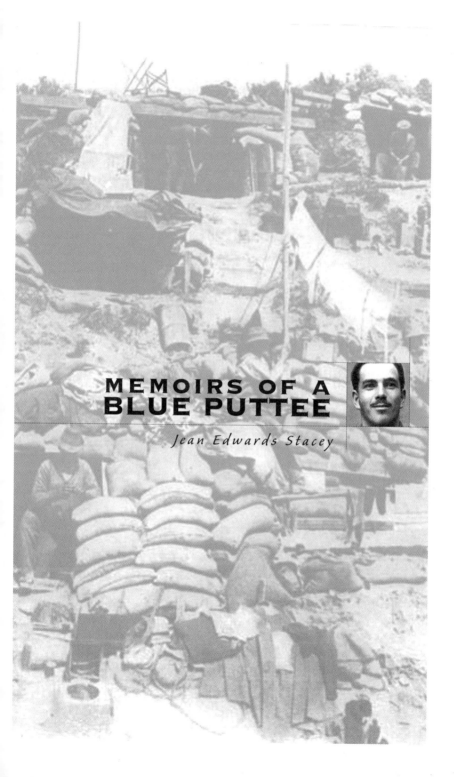

MEMOIRS OF A
BLUE PUTTEE

Jean Edwards Stacey

Published by:
DRC Publishers
3 Parliament Street
St. John's, Newfoundland
A1A 2Y6
phone: (709) 726-0960
e-mail staceypj@avint.net

National Library of Canada Cataloguing in Publication

Stacey, A.J. (Anthony James) 1890-1969
Memoirs of a Blue Puttee: The Newfoundland Regiment in the First World War/A.J. Stacey and Jean Edwards Stacey

Includes bibliographical references
ISBN 0-9684209-1-5

1. Stacey, A.J. (Anthony James), 1890-1969. 2. World War, 1914-1918 - Personal narratives, Newfoundland.3. Great Britain. Army, Newfoundland Regiment - Biography. 4. World War, 1914-1918 - Regimental histories - Newfoundland. I. Stacey, Jean Edwards II. Title

D640.S69 2002   940.4'81718   C2002-902452-8

Printed in Newfoundland

Design by Sarah Hansen
Cover photo hand-coloured by Paula Tizzard.

The author would like to thank Tom Dale and Ken Simmons for their advice and help.

Table of Contents

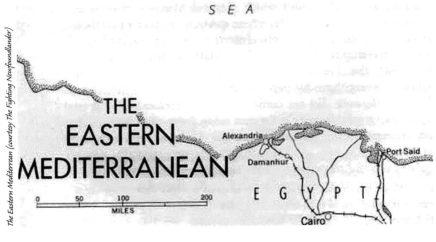

foreword

This book has been a long time in the making. My husband Peter's father, Anthony James Stacey, was a veteran of the first World War, indeed he was a Blue Puttee, one of the famous First Five Hundred volunteers in the Newfoundland Regiment.

He wrote his memoirs of the First World War in longhand during the 1960s and they were typed up by a daughter-in-law, Rose, wife of his son, Robert.

The memoirs were later re-typed by Mr. Stacey's grand-daughter, Cheryl Stacey, daughter of his son, Bruce. Typing the memoirs made them easier to read, but it wasn't until Mr. Stacey's sons, Cecil and Harold, got to work and put their dad's writing into chapter form with some additional information about the war that I truly got interested in doing anything further.

Spurred on by my husband, who is the tenth of Jim and Blanche Stacey's 12 children, I began working on the basis of what Cecil and Harold had done.

What I did essentially was take the memoirs written by Mr. Stacey and add as full a history as I could of World War I and the Newfoundland Regiment.

Anthony James Stacey died in 1969 and I'm sorry that he didn't get to see the final results of his work. I can only hope that it would have met with his approval.

This book is dedicated to all veterans of war, including my own dad, Martin Edwards of Gander, who served overseas with the RAF 125 Newfoundland Squadron during the Second World War.

I hope you, as the reader, will enjoy reading Memoirs of a Blue Puttee and finding out more about about the Newfoundland Regiment and the First World War. I know you will as well occasionally chuckle as you read Mr. Stacey's reminiscences for even in war there is humour and laughter.

— Jean Edwards Stacey

The Caribou at Beaumont-Hamel.
Photo courtesy of John Edward FitzGerald, 2001.

❉ *chapter one*

J uly 1, celebrated as Canada Day, is a day of mixed emotions for the people of Newfoundland and Labrador. The joy of a nation-wide party is tinged with sadness as people recall the men of the Newfoundland Regiment who died in a First World War battle at Beaumont Hamel, France, on July 1, 1916.

In this province, not all that long ago, July 1 was known as Memorial Day and people fastened tiny floral bouquets of blue and white forget-me-nots to their lapels in memory of those who gave their lives in a battle some refer to as the July Drive.

Of all the places where Newfoundland soldiers fought in two World Wars, no other name means as much to Newfoundlanders as Beaumont Hamel. The casualty lists from that battle reached into almost every community of what was then an island colony of Britain.

There were 801 men of the Newfoundland Regiment who took part in the July Drive. The final grim figures revealing the virtual annihilation of the regiment gave a count of 233 killed or died of wounds, 386 wounded and 91 missing.

For the Newfoundland Regiment, Beaumont Hamel was their first engagement in France and the costliest of the First World War. When the roll call of those not wounded was taken the day after the battle, only 68 answered their name.

Among those who were at Beaumont Hamel that day and lived to talk and write about it was then Private, later Sergeant, Anthony James (Jim) Stacey, of the Newfoundland Regiment.

His regimental number was 466 and he had the distinction of being a Blue Puttee, the name proudly worn by the First 500 volunteers for service overseas.

In 1916, he was 25 years old.

Saturday, July 1, 1916, marked the opening day of the Battle of the Somme when 100,000 Allied soldiers set out on the "Big Push" – a colossal infantry offensive along a roughly 25 mile stretch of the Western front called the Somme. Expectations were the troops would smash through the German defenses and clear a path for the cavalry to advance to the Channel coast.

Beginning soon after daylight, the attacking soldiers climbed out of their trenches and marched as ordered, slowly, wave upon wave, with bayonets held high.

Each man was burdened with roughly 70 pounds of equipment, including shovels, wire-cutters and sections of bridges which, once assembled, would enable passage across enemy trenches.

The Germans had, however, been long forewarned of an infantry assault.

To make matters worse, the Allied artillery siege which had been aimed at the enemy throughout the preceding weeks had missed most of its targets. It had not destroyed the enemy's guns, the bulk of their substantial barbed wire defenses nor the deep dug-outs which concealed scores of platoons. The heavily burdened Allied soldiers quickly became easy targets for the readied German guns.

With the advancing Allied forces there was a sole infantry battalion from Newfoundland. Raised within just two months of Great Britain's declaration of war, it had already fought with distinction in Gallipoli.

One of four battalions of the 29th Division's 88th Brigade, the Newfoundland Regiment was assigned a role with the second attacking wave.

At 7:30 a.m. platoons from the 87th Brigade were to set out to capture the first two lines of German fortification at Beaumont Hamel. The Newfoundland Regiment, together with a battalion from the Essex Regiment, were to take the third enemy line 70 minutes later. It was assumed they would face little opposition.

Little, however, went according to plan. A huge mine was ignited under a German trench at 7:20 a.m. Although it destroyed its intended target, the blast also alerted the enemy to the impending infantry attack. German soldiers prepared to defend their lines. German artillerymen countered by shelling Allied ground.

At 7:30 a.m. in the face of this military barrage, the 87th Brigade embarked.

At 8:45 a.m. the Newfoundland Regiment and the Essex Regiment were ordered to provide them with support. By this time, the forward trenches were so clogged with bodies and debris that the advance of the Essex regiment was delayed, and the Newfoundlanders were left to cross about 1,000 yards of exposed front independently.

From their starting position in the St. John's Road trench, few made it to the beginning of the Allied barbed wire entanglements, 250 yards away.

Those who managed to get to the barbed wire had to make their way through previously cut zigzag openings which were well covered by German guns.

If they made it through the gaps and emerged into what was known as No Man's Land, they could look down an incline and see that at least 550 yards of open ground lay between them and the fully intact first line of German defense.

Halfway down the slope an isolated tree marked an area where the enemy's shrapnel was particularly deadly. Called "The Danger Tree",its twisted skeleton has been preserved and still stands at the spot where so many soldiers fell. Some of the Newfoundlanders progressed far enough to hurl bombs at the enemy trenches, but most were struck down long before that point. Many were killed at the start, as they clambered out of their trenches. Less than half an hour after it began, the Battle of Beaumont Hamel was over.

The Commanding Officer, who had watched the destruction of his regiment from a support trench, reported to Brigade headquarters that the attack had failed.

By the time the battle ended, little remained of the 801 men of the Newfoundland Regiment. Casualties numbered more than 700, one-third of which were fatal. Only 68 escaped serious injury.

For the British Army, July 1 was the bloodiest day of World War I. They suffered 57,470 casualties. German dead or wounded totaled 8,000.

Full news of the tragedy didn't arrive in Newfoundland until July 13. Members of the clergy then began what seemed an endless succession of condolence visits.

During the First World War, Jim Stacey was one of the Newfoundland Regiment's four battalion runners. The job of a battalion runner was to deliver messages to company commanders, medical officers, transport sections and Brigade headquarters.

On the morning of July 1, 1916, his orders were to bring the message to advance, or go over the top, to Captain Bruce Reid of B company and Captain Eric Ayre of D Company.

Less than half an hour after the message was delivered, the Newfoundland Regiment was almost annihilated. In memoirs, written years after the war ended, Jim described the sight of heaps of khaki slumped on the ground and muddy trenches filled with the dead and dying.

All of the officers who went forward in the Newfoundland attack were either wounded or killed.

Captain Eric Ayre was one of four members of his family who lost their lives that day. Two of his cousins, Gerald and Wilfrid Ayre, both lieutenants in the Newfoundland Regiment, were killed within yards of him. His only brother, Captain Bernard Ayre, lost his life serving with the Norfolk Regiment at nearby Maricourt.

Reporting on the efforts of the Newfoundland Regiment following the Battle of Beaumont Hamel, Major-General Sir Beauvoir de Lisle, Commander of the 29th Division, wrote that it was a magnificent display of trained and disciplined valor, and its assault failed because dead men could advance no further.

Following the end of the First World War, the Newfoundland government purchased the 40 acres of land over which the Newfoundland Regiment advanced at Beaumont Hamel.

The area became a memorial park. On the highest point, overlooking the site of St. John's Road and the slopes beyond, a bronze caribou, the emblem of the Newfoundland Regiment, was erected. In 1960, the work of reconstructing a representative portion of the British and German trenches was begun. The work was completed a year later, on the 45th anniversary of the battle.

Jim Stacey was among those who were at Beaumont Hamel in 1961. He traveled to France with then Newfoundland premier, Joseph Smallwood, who was there to unveil a bronze plaque listing the battle honourss won by the Newfoundland Regiment and paying tribute to the fallen. ✸

▨ *chapter two*

The Newfoundland Regiment, which was formed at the beginning of the First World War, was not the first to bear that name. Enrolment of the first body of troops to bear the name "Newfoundland" occurred in 1779, when Capt. Robert Pringle, the military commander of St. John's, acting on the orders of Governor Richard Edwards, established a defensive force, His Majesty's Newfoundland Regiment of Foot. The Regiment consisted of three companies of 100 men, each company commanded by a captain, a lieutenant, a second lieutenant, and an ensign.

Pringle, as commanding officer, was given the rank of lieutenant-colonel.

At this time in Newfoundland's history, work on fortifications put in place in St. John's at the outbreak of the American Revolution were well underway.

Fort Townshend, begun in 1775, was nearly complete and Military Road was being constructed to connect it with Fort William, on the site of the present day Fairmont Newfoundland hotel.

To accommodate the new regiment, the old barracks at Fort William were hastily repaired. As well, uniforms were requisitioned from England.

Regimental uniforms consisted of a blue coat, with red lapels and cuffs. Waistcoats and breeches were white and hats were laced with white worsted. Drummers wore red coats.

Up until 1783, when the Treaty of Paris ended hostilities between England, France and the new Republic of the United States of America, the Newfoundland Regiment of Foot stood guard in St. John's, concerned always about rumours of a possible invasion from the Americans and their French allies.

As is evident in the following extracts from an orderly book kept by Lieutenant John Dun, commanding officer Pringle frequently had concerns about the behaviour of his troops.

Dun's entry for February 28, 1780:

Colonel Pringle is sorry to observe that notwithstanding the number that have been forgiven drunkenness, many of them still persist in that beastly and unsoldier-like custom, and as lenience or easiness will not reform them, it is therefore his intention to bring the first offender to publick punishment that none may plead ignorance, particularly as the muster they are about to receive may lead many of them into temptation.

Entry for March 26, 1780:

Snooks, of Capt. Graham's Company to be interred this afternoon without Military Honours, as by his own indiscretion of love of Liquor he brought himself so suddenly to his Grave. The Colonel begs that those men of the Regiment who are addicted to that vice will take a warning from his untimely fate and resolve to refrain from a Sin that will infallibly bring them to disgrace in this world and perhaps to hell in the next.

The return of peace ended the need for maintaining the Newfoundland Regiment as part of the garrison of St. John's. On October 5, 1783, the unit was formally disbanded.

Ten years later, in 1793, with the outbreak of the French Revolution, Britain found herself at war with France and King George 111 authorized the raising of the Royal Newfoundland Regiment of Foot, a unit of 600 infantry which was to serve only in North America.

Fears of an enemy invasion of Newfoundland seemed imminent in September of 1796 when a large French fleet, under the command of Admiral Richery, appeared off the narrows of St. John's and threatened to attack the town. With clever positioning of limited troops and ships, then Governor James Wallace was able to carry out such a successful bluff that he managed to convince the French that St. John's was too heavily defended to attack.

Much to everyone's relief, the French fleet sailed away after three days.

In 1800, when the garrison in St. John's was under the command of Brigadier-General John Skerrett, there was a mutiny which involved member of the Newfoundland Regiment.

Many of the Regiment's Irish recruits were in sympathy with, or members of, the United Irishmen Society (UIS), an organization founded in Ireland by Wolfe Tone in 1791. The Society's aim of ending English rule in Ireland ultimately led to the Irish Rebellion of 1798 and the deaths of some 30,000 Irishmen killed by British troops.

Like their fellow countrymen, Irish soldiers in Newfoundland felt they were being subjected to oppression. Fed up with poor living conditions and denial of political and religious freedom, they planned a revolt for April 20 which, in the opinion of many, was to have seen the assassination of officers of the Regiment as well as the merchants of St. John's.

Forewarned of the plot by Catholic Bishop James O'Donel, Skerrett managed to capture the mutineers before they carried out their plan.

Five of the Irish soldiers were sentenced to be hung immediately, the other 11 were ordered sent to Halifax to be tried for treason by the Duke of Kent.

Following the trial in Halifax, three of the men were hung, the remaining eight had their death sentences commuted.

The mutiny of 1800, and the subsequent Treaty of Amiens that was signed between England and France, led to the disbandment of the Newfoundland Regiment on July 31, 1802.

A year later, faced with the threat of renewed hostilities with the French and Dutch, Skerrett received orders to raise a regiment of 10 companies to be called the Newfoundland Regiment of Fencible Infantry.

In 1805, Skerrett was given permission to call his troops the Royal Newfoundland Regiment.

In 1812, following a declaration of war between England and the United States of America, and with American troops poised to attack Canada, the Royal Newfoundland Regiment was dispatched to Quebec where they remained on garrison duty for the next four and a half years.

During the War of 1812, the Royal Newfoundland Regiment fought and died in almost every major engagement in Upper Canada.

The War of 1812 was officially ended by the Treaty of Ghent, an agreement signed by the United States and Great Britain in Ghent, Belgium, on Dec. 24, 1814.

For a year and a half after the end of the war, the Royal Newfoundland Regiment formed the garrison at St. John's, but attempts to bring it up to full force had little success.

In October, 1815, the unit consisted of 23 officers and 315 other ranks. In June 1816, the Regiment was disbanded. It would be almost 100 years before it would be resurrected.

Great Britain maintained a garrison in Newfoundland for more than 54 years after the Royal Newfoundland Regiment was disbanded in 1816.

The use of regular regiments ended in 1825 when the 60th Regiment, the third of three infantry battalions to serve at St. John's in the period immediately following the Treaty of Ghent, was withdrawn. Its place was taken by the Royal Veteran Companies, three companies later reduced to two, which was made up of former servicemen and renamed the Royal Newfoundland Veteran Companies in 1828.

In 1843, the two companies became the Royal Newfoundland Companies.

In 1862, they were absorbed into the Royal Canadian Rifle Regiment. This colonial unit, which from then on supplied the infantry for the St. John's garrison, had been formed in 1841 from older men of the 19 British regiments which were at the time serving in Canada. The unit's principal duty was to prevent desertion to the United States.

Fourteen companies of the Royal Canadian Rifles were engaged in preventing desertion. The two companies in Newfoundland, about 300 strong, garrisoned St. John's until 1870.

Early in 1869, Britain served notice it could no longer maintain large establishments of troops overseas to garrison self-governing colonies. This included Newfoundland, which had been granted Responsible Government in 1855.

In 1870, Britain gave formal notification it would no longer maintain a garrison in Newfoundland. That fall, the Royal Canadian Rifles were disbanded and the government of the colony proceeded with plans for a constabulary to maintain law and order. Attempts on more than one occasion to form a militia for Newfoundland's defense failed.

Newfoundland, an island colony separated by water from potential enemies and protected as well by the British Navy, had no real need of a permanent military force in the absence of war.

And, burdened as the colony was with financial difficulties, no political party would seriously consider large peacetime expenditures on armaments.

So it was that in 1899, at the outbreak of the Boer War, when soldiers from all over the British Empire were being sent to fight in South Africa, the Governor of Newfoundland, Sir Henry McCallum, had to express his regret that England's oldest colony was unable to be represented for the simple reason that no trained forces were available.

A move towards military preparedness in peacetime came at the close of the Boer War when Governor Cavendish Boyle undertook to form a Royal Naval Reserve of 600 men.

Five years later, a proposal to organize a reserve force on land fell by the wayside.

Prior to 1914, these were the last attempts to establish a military force in Newfoundland.

For the remaining years of peace, exchanges between the colony and London were limited to questions of supplying rifles and ammunition for use in training cadet corps. ✸

*Jim Stacey left his native England and
came to Newfoundland in 1911.*

 chapter three

Jim Stacey was born in Benson, South Oxfordshire, on November 17, 1890. A young man with an adventurous streak, he left his native England in 1911 and traveled by ship to Newfoundland where it had been arranged he would stay with his brother, Charles, who had been in the British colony since 1903, and worked at the Bank of Montreal in the capital city of St. John's.

Shortly after he arrived in St. John's, Jim got a job with the firm of George Knowling in the groceries and provisions store on Water Street, earning $24 a month.

After six months with the Knowling firm, Jim left for a new job with the Reid Newfoundland Railway, which started a daily service of six trains a week from St. John's to Port aux Basques June 1, 1912. Jim was hired as a waiter in the dining car. He worked with the railway up until 1914 when he became one of the first to volunteer to serve with the Newfoundland Regiment in the First World War.

Jim began his memoirs of the First World War with his joining up in St. John's:

When you have shouted Rule Britannia,
And you have sung God Save the Queen,
And you have finished killing Kruger
With your mouth

This is the beginning of a patriotic song, which I remember from the beginning of the century, when only a youth of nine years, at the start of the Boer war. This seemed to me the trend of things, as there was always a new war, just as peace was reached on the latter one.

In spite of the fact that my father joined the regular army twice, he never encouraged me to join. Father was in a military unit for home defense, "The Volunteers"; later they changed it to the "Territorials" and each summer they would go to camp for six weeks training.

When war was declared in 1914, there was much singing of patriotic songs and flag waving, which seemed to be needed to whip up emotion since "enlistment" relied mainly on volunteers. That was the spirit that dominated. It was "your duty" in the hour of need. The Government asked for only five hundred volunteers and on September 2nd my mind was made up. I decided to enlist. I went to the C.L.B. Armoury where Dr. Wakefield gave me a medical examination. Knowing that I had fallen arches, I was careful to brace my feet up by pointing my toes in. I passed the exam and was enlisted. (No.466). We camped at Pleasantville and were given khaki drill uniforms and blue puttees. The latter were used by the Church Lads Brigade, and they had a stock of them on hand. Headdress could be anything and generally was what was worn when enlisting. As time went on, I made a special effort to get on the list of the "Five Hundred" and for the next month it was quite a picnic. There were Mothers, coming down to Headquarters, saying that their sons, who had joined up, were under age. It was a mix up and remained so until we reached the other side. Church parade on Sunday was all I knew of military discipline. Dr. Patterson, Major of the Regiment, formerly a doctor with the Reid Newfoundland Company Railway knew me as a waiter in the Railway's dining car and picked me for duty in the Officer's mess. This was my assignment until we sailed for England.

On Saturday, October 3, 1914, the citizens of St. John's lined the streets to watch as the first contingent of the Newfoundland Regiment marched in columns of four out of their camp in Pleasantville, through the streets of the city and finally down the steep hill to Water Street and the Furness Withy Company's wharf, where the SS Florizel was waiting to take them overseas.

Governor Walter Davidson and his wife, along with Prime Minister Edward Morris, were at the pier to bid the Regiment farewell. On the dock as well were the bands of the Church Lads Brigade, the Methodist Guards and the Salvation Army.

There was tremendous applause as Lieutenant Bert Tait, accompanied by a guard with fixed bayonets, marched on board the Florizel with the regimental colours.

By 6 p.m. all members of the Regiment were aboard.

The Florizel cast off and steamed out into the harbour accompanied by the strains of "Auld Lang Syne" and "God Be With You Till We Meet Again." [1]

All next day, the Florizel lay at anchor in St. John's Harbour, waiting to rendezvous with the Canadian Contingent, which was due to pass within 50 miles of St. John's.

At 10 p.m. on October 4, the master of the Florizel, Captain William Martin, ordered the anchor hoisted and the vessel steamed slowly out through the Narrows into the Atlantic and headed southward.

The departure of the First 500 volunteers came just two months from the day that war had been declared.

On October 5, The Evening Telegram described the departure of the Newfoundland Regiment:

The largest gathering of citizens ever seen here assembled on Saturday afternoon to witness the embarkation of the First Newfoundland Regiment. All business was suspended and almost the entire population turned out to view the finest procession of the finest men seen here for many years.

The volunteers, under command of Captain Franklin and headed by the Catholic Cadet Corps Band, left the camp at 4:30 p.m. and proceeded by way of Kings Bridge, Circular, Bannerman and Military Roads, Prescott and Water Streets to the Furness Withy Company's pier where the transport Florizel lay waiting.

Thousands marched from the camp with them and as they moved through the line of route citizens joined the ranks and stepped to the music of the grand patriotic air rendered by the Band. Very many people were assembled all along the line of march, and cheered the soldiers as they swung along to the strain of martial music. With a buoyant step and a cheerful face they exchanged greetings showered on them from every side, from mothers and fathers, wives and sweethearts, old men and women, and even some babes in arms, who waved their little hands in farewell to the friends who used to speak kindly to them, and of whom their little children's hearts felt proud.

The true spirit of patriotism was everywhere and at intervals from out the din of cheering came a weak voiced "Goodbye my son. God bless you." It was perhaps the farewell of some mother who had given all for the defense of the Empire.

The article ended: *We wish the 500 volunteers God speed, good luck and a safe return."* ❈

Jim Stacey, shortly after enlisting.

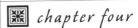 *chapter four*

In the summer of 1914, when people in Newfoundland picked up their newspapers they read that England's attempt to settle the Irish question by giving Home Rule was meeting strenuous opposition from Ulster. They read that suffragettes were trying to keep in the public eye through so called "nuisance" tactics as they fought for votes for women and that, in France, a cabinet minister's wife was on trial for having shot the editor of Le Figaro

There had been another shooting as well, but it didn't garner too many headlines on this side of the Atlantic. On June 28, in Sarajevo, capital of the Austro-Hungarian province of Bosnia, a Serb nationalist named Gavrilo Princip assassinated Archduke Francis Ferdinand, heir presumptive to the throne of Austria-Hungary.

A month later, this shooting ignited an international conflagration.

On July 28, Austria Hungary declared war on Serbia.

Tension between the two armed camps into which the major powers of Europe had aligned themselves rapidly increased to the breaking point.

On July 30, Russia, avowed protector of the Slav people, began to mobilize.

On August 1, when the Czar of Russia ignored German Emperor William's demand for a halt of these warlike preparations, Germany declared war on Russia.

As Germany ordered mobilization, France did the same.

On August 2, the German minister to Brussels served an ultimatum demanding free passage through Belgium territory for German troops attacking France. Germany appeared to be conveniently ignoring the fact that Belgium neutrality was guaranteed by an 1839 treaty which had been signed by France, Britain and Germany itself.

During the anxious days after the assassination in Sarajevo, Great Britain had made repeated efforts to preserve peace but now there seemed only one decision. On the morning of August 4, as news came of a German violation of Belgium soil, the British Foreign Secretary, Sir Edward Grey, sent an ultimatum giving Germany until midnight to withdraw its troops from Belgium.

That evening, as dusk fell on London and with no word forthcoming from Germany, Sir Edward stood by the window in his office and said despairingly,

The lights are going out all over Europe. We shall not see them lit again in our lifetime. [2]

When Britain's ultimatum to Germany passed without a satisfactory reply, Britain was at war with Germany.

It was 9:25 p.m. on August 4 when the message from the Secretary of State for the Colonies was received in St. John's and immediately passed to Government House.

The message said simply:

War has broken out with Germany.

What was later termed the Great War became a global conflict involving more than 30 countries.

Aligned with Britain were the 28 nations of the Allied Powers, including France, Russia and Italy and, in 1917, the United States.

The Allies, as they were called, opposed the coalition known as the Central Power, consisting of Austria-Hungary, Germany, Turkey and Bulgaria.

In 1914, Newfoundland was a colony of Great Britain with no existing military, but with a number of para-military groups: the Church Lads Brigade (CLB), the Catholic Cadet Corps, the Newfoundland Highlanders, the Methodist Guards and the Legion of Frontiersmen, which had branches in St. John's, northern Newfoundland and Labrador.

All of these groups provided many of the early enlistments for the Newfoundland Regiment, which was formed shortly after war was declared.

One member of the CLB, Thomas Ricketts, only 15 when he lied about his age in order to enlist in the Newfoundland Regiment, won the Victoria Cross, the highest British military honour, for his actions in clearing a German gun battery on October 14, 1918. When he returned home after the war, then Sgt. Ricketts received a hero's welcome from proud Newfoundlanders, including a tour of St. John's in an open carriage pulled by loyal admirers.

The night the Newfoundland Regiment held its first recruitment meeting, members of the Catholic Cadet Corps marched in a body to the CLB Armoury, which had been designated Regimental headquarters. Captains George Carty, Gus O' Brien, Michael Summers and Laurence Murphy immediately offered their services.

They were soon followed by 160 other members of the Corps. Twenty-four members of the Bell Island company also volunteered.

When the First 500 embarked for Great Britain, the Catholic Cadet Corps was well represented in their ranks. In early November, 1915, two members of the Corps won high honourss for their bravery in Gallipoli.

Lieutenant James Donnelly became the first officer of the Newfoundland Regiment to win the Military Cross, while Sergeant William Gladney of Bell Island, was first to win the Distinguished Conduct Medal.

In Battle Harbour, Labrador, when he heard that war had broken out, Dr. Arthur Wakefield, a former member of the Royal Army Medical Corps who served for many years on the hospital staff of the Grenfell Mission and was, at the time, the officer in charge of the Newfoundland Command of the Legion of Frontiersmen, hurried to St. John's to offer some 150 Frontiersmen for active service overseas.

A large number of Frontiersmen were early volunteers with the Newfoundland Regiment and were to serve in it with distinction overseas. ✸

Soldiers of the Newfoundland Regiment practicing target shooting in Pleasantville
(Courtesy The Trail of the Caribou)

 chapter five

The First Newfoundland Regiment comprising A and B companies was organized in August 1914. On August 21, Governor Walter Davidson issued a proclamation calling on men between the ages of 19 and 36 to enlist in the First Newfoundland Regiment for services abroad for the duration of the war, but not exceeding one year.

Men were recruited for active service under the following conditions, as stated by the Office of the First Newfoundland Regiment.

1. After they have passed the Medical Examination and been finally accepted by the Recruiting Officer at St. John's, they will be sworn in and undergo training until such time as it is decided to send the contingent abroad.

2. Pay will be at the rate of One Dollar per day, and ten cents per day field allowance, and will begin as soon as the men are sworn in. While in St. John's, the men will find board and lodging for themselves, and an allowance of fifty cents per day will be made to them on this account, in addition to the pay as above.

3. Free transportation will be provided from all Outports to St. John's on an order from the Magistrates to recruits who have passed local Medical Examination.

4. At the present time single men only are required between the ages of 19 and 36, not less than five feet three inches in height, chest average 34 inches, weight 120 lbs.

For further information, those interested in applying were told to see the nearest Magistrate or the Recruiting Officer in St. John's.

The response was immediate.

On August 21, when enrolment opened at the CLB Armoury, 74 volunteers signed up the first night. Within a week, 275 men had been enroled.

All recruits had to pass a medical exam by a team of eight doctors headed by Captain Cluny MacPherson, a former Surgeon-General of the Methodist Guards Brigade, and head of the St. John Ambulance Brigade in Newfoundland.

Recruits soon began arriving from the outports and enrolment continued to be brisk.

By September 2, the number of recruits had risen to 743, of whom 250 had passed the medical exam and been sworn in.

The next step was to set up a camp for accommodating and training the troops.

The newly formed Patriotic Association of Newfoundland chose Crown Land in Pleasantville, on the north shore of Quidi Vidi Lake, as the site for a training camp.

The city brigades provided 47 tents, Governor Davidson sent three marquees from Government House, an additional 50 smaller tents were provided by local businesses and citizens, and the Anglo-Newfoundland Development Company in Grand Falls provided wooden tent floors free of charge.

When the first 120 recruits marched into Pleasantville on September 2, they had adequate living quarters. Making sure the men were well fed was the responsibility of Camp Quartermaster and Equipment Officer, Captain Herbert Outerbridge.

After an urgent call to London brought word that the British War Office was unable to provide neither uniforms nor the cloth with which to make them, the Patriotic Association's Equipment Committee quickly commissioned local clothing manufacturers to produce fatigue uniforms consisting of tunics and pants of khaki drill.

At the time soldiers used long strips of material, called puttees, to wrap their legs from ankle to knee for protection and support. Since no khaki woolen material suitable for making puttees was available, the recruits at Pleasantville ended up with puttees of navy blue.

The only Newfoundland soldiers to wear these were the members of the First Contingent of the Newfoundland Regiment who left St. John's in October, 1914.

The blue puttees became a badge of distinction, and the soldiers who wore them were known as Blue Puttees.

To be a Blue Puttee was to be a member of the famous First 500.

Once the new recruits were sworn in, training began in earnest. The daily routine at Pleasantville included arms drill, foot drill, "skirmishing" and marching.

Rifle practice started without delay. Recruits were classified according to their familiarity with rifles. The most experienced were taken in squads of 64 to a range on the South Side Hill. Novices were given firing practice at the miniature ranges of the brigade armories in the city. The sessions on the South Side Hills were carried out with old Long Lee-Enfield rifles and ammunition from HMS Calypso, the training ship of the Royal Naval Reservists.

By the end of the second week of September, there were 492 volunteers under canvas, only eight short of the 500 Governor Davidson had promised Britain he would immediately supply to the war effort.

The full complement of 500 was in place by October.

In Newfoundland, during the week preceding the declaration of war, Governor Davidson had received a series of cablegrams from the Colonial Office in London keeping him abreast of what was happening in Europe.

On July 29, officials in Britain sent a warning signal to all Dominions and Colonies: Adopt precautionary stage. Names of powers will be communicated later if necessary.

There followed messages with instructions to call out the Royal Naval Reserve, and to establish censorship on the island.

Governor Davidson proclaimed censorship on August 3, and that same evening the Prime Minister, Sir Edward Morris, called at Government House to confer with the governor, who was very concerned about Newfoundland being defenseless.

When England declared war on Germany on August 4, Newfoundland was the least prepared of its overseas possessions to supply trained soldiers and equipment.

There was some degree of preparedness as far as the navy was concerned, because for 10 years prior to the war the Royal Naval Reserve had engaged in training small groups of volunteers. The volunteers underwent training on a vessel in St. John's harbor and later had a six-month cruise at sea with the North Atlantic squadron of the British Navy.

At the time war was declared, however, the Royal Naval Reserve had no more than 70 Reservists at hand. The rest were away fishing.

As it stood, the reservists were the sole military force of any kind in the colony.

London had sounded a warning about the necessity of being on guard against a possible attack prior to a formal declaration of war. As well, the British Admiralty reported that the German cruiser, Dresden, was near the French island of St. Pierre, no more than 250 miles by sea from St. John's.

The Governor immediately made plans. He wrote in his daily log that if the Dresden entered St. John's harbor, citizens would block the entrance to the narrows with two ships that they would sink. If the German ship threatened retaliation, he said citizens of the city would "exact the fullest retribution on the whole crew." If, however, the ship surrendered, the safety and personal effects of the officers and men would be guaranteed, they would be transported to neutral territory, and the ship would not be sunk or blown up.

The information about the Dresden proved incorrect. St. John's wasn't in danger, but Davidson continued to be anxious to do what he could to help the war effort.

On August 8, following a meeting of the Executive Council at Government House, he cabled London:

Authority is desired by my Ministers to enlist special men for service abroad by land and sea. Ministers undertake to raise force of Naval Reserve by the 31st of October to one thousand efficient men available for naval service abroad for one year, and are willing to meet all local expenses. Several hundred with efficient local brigade training offer for enlistment for land service abroad. Five hundred could, I believe, be enlisted within one month. Propose to induce serviceable men between eighteen and thirty-six to enlist for training for home defense wherever corps instruction available. Material for further drafts would be formed by these.

A reply came the next day:

His Majesty's Government gladly accepts the offer of the Newfoundland Government to raise troops for service abroad. Will telegraph later as to Naval Reserve. [3]

The British Admiralty accepted the proposal to increase the Royal Naval Reserve to 1, 000 on August 14, and the first steps to make good the initial offer of 500 soldiers was taken at a meeting held August 10. The meeting was held in the office of the Colonial Secretary, John Bennett, and presided over by the Prime Minister.

In attendance were representatives from each of the city brigades, the Legion of Frontiersmen, and the St. John's Rifle Club, as well as the commanding officer of HMS Calypso, the training shop of the Royal Naval Reservists, and the Inspector General of the Newfoundland Police. Arrangements were made for a general meeting to be held the following

Wednesday evening.

On Wednesday, August 14, an enthusiastic group of citizens packed the CLB Armoury.

In support of the government's actions, they passed resolutions authorizing the Governor's appointment of a committee of 25 citizens to set about enlisting and equipping the 500 troops promised to Britain, as well as men to be enrolled for training for home defense.

The meeting marked the beginning of the Newfoundland Patriotic Committee, later to be called the Patriotic Association of Newfoundland.

For the next three years, the association carried out the task of raising, equipping, transporting and caring for the land contingents sent from Newfoundland to Britain.

Although the Royal Naval Reserve made a substantial contribution to the colony's war effort by providing approximately 2,000 volunteers, their dispersal throughout the British Royal Navy meant they did not have a group identity. It was with the Newfoundland Regiment that Newfoundlanders found their sense of identity. ✪

chapter six

On September 1, 1914, The Evening Telegram listed the names of 597 men who had volunteered to serve in the Newfoundland Regiment. It was noted only 350 of those had passed a doctor's examination and been pronounced fit for foreign service.

It was reported that 30 young men from Bell Island had volunteered for service, as well as three from Grand Falls.

The paper said a total of $15,310 had been contributed to the Patriotic Fund. There was news as well of the formation of the Ladies Patriotic Association.

At a meeting convened by Lady Davidson, 700 women expressed their willingness to assist in aiding the Empire by providing necessities for the soldiers at the Front.

President of the newly formed Ladies Patriotic Assocation was Lady Davidson; vice presidents were Lady Morris, Lady Horwood and Mrs. Pitts. Mrs. Cluny McPherson was secretary and Mrs. George Emerson was treasurer.

Advertisements in The Evening Telegram on September 1, 1914, included smart, stylish suits for men and women at J. J. Strong; safety razors at Chesley Woods and scythes, potato hooks and hay rakes in the hardware department at Bowring Brothers.

Hendersons on Theatre Hill was selling ladies sample dresses for $2.98.

Harvey & Company were promoting passenger rates from Montreal to and from St. John's priced at $15, one way, or $25 return.

C. P. Eagan was advertising a fresh supply of Irish butter, one pound blocks and bulk.

Martin Hardware Co. announced they had a new shipment of Ross Rifles.

Steer Bros. advertised the arrival of Ladies Famous Bernalde Shoes for $2 a pair.

Marshall Bros. advised women who sewed to come in early to get their dress material.

The Holloway Studio located on the corner of Henry Street and Bates Hill promised to develop films and make prints of pictures in 24 hours. Prints made on postcards were 65 cents a dozen.

At the Nickel Theatre, the feature film was *The Sign of the Black Lily*.

At the Crescent, it was *Robispierre*, a dramatization of the most stirring incidents of the French Revolution.

On September 1, The Evening Telegram published a poem Rose Greene of Bell Island had written especially for those who had volunteered to serve with the Newfoundland Regiment.

Your country needs you!
Now what answer comes?
Roll after roll of deafening battle drums
And shells and cannons with war's bloody strife
And all the dangers with which war is rife
Are crowding up before each eager sight
And Heaven itself seems calling "Fight for Right.

The poem ended with a blessing,

Because they call dear England Motherland
And on dear Terra Nova's hill they stand
Because the Union Jack floats free above
They go to battle for the land they love
God bless and keep their souls and courage bright.
And keep them for their country strong in might.

The September 1 paper had announcements of school openings. Bishop Spencer College was due to open September 8, the East End

School on September 7 and Bishop Field College on September 9.

Dicks & Co. Ltd. had school supplies for sale.

Two shops, F. Smallwood and Parker & Monroe, were promoting a sale of boys and girls shoes.

There was a stern warning that berry pickers should stay away from the Southside Hill as the rifle range there was in constant use from daylight to dark for musketry practice until the Regiment departed for England.

In war news, it was reported that $50 million worth of German shipping had been seized and taken to British ports.

There was news as well of what were called Horrible Atrocities.

Following a battle near Diest on August 12, the Belgian government charged that German troops had shot Major Von Donne through his head as he lay helplessly wounded, and then burnt his body.

When Von Domme's body was disinterred, a total of 26 bullets were found in his head.

The Belgian government accused the Germans of torturing an elderly man with fire and finally burning him to death.

A brief from London noted the first 100,000 recruits who had responded to Field Marshal Kitchener's appeal for volunteers had gone into training in Great Britain.

As Britain's Secretary of State for War, Kitchener had quickly foreseen the war was likely to be a prolonged affair and would require huge numbers of volunteers. The famous poster with Kitchener's martial image and pointing finger with the caption "Your country needs you" was chosen to inspire volunteers and it worked wonderfully well.

By the end of 1914, a total of 1,186,000 men had come forward to offer their services.

On September 1, The Evening Telegram reported that Berlin had announced mobilization of the Turkish Army: It is said the Turkish government will form an army of the first line composed of 200, 000 men, all Mohammedans.

On September 15, there was news of a great Russian victory against the Germans.

In a battle lasting 17 days, the Russians had captured 180,000 prisoners, 450 field guns, 1,000 fortress artillery, 4,000 transport wagons and seven airplanes.

A column titled London Gossip mentioned the arrival at Charing Cross Station of large numbers of French and Belgian refugees.

On September 18, it was reported that Lord Kitchener had declared the tide of war was turning in favour of the Allies. Kitchener said while the struggle was bound to be a long one, England could look forward to the final outcome with quiet confidence

News from Germany was that Prince Frederick William of Lepple had taken his own life following a mistake of his regiment in Liege, Belgium, on August 4. In the dark of night, the German cavalry regiment had mistaken a German infantry regiment for Belgians with deadly results. Prince Frederick, fearing to face the anger of the German emperor in the aftermath of what is now called "friendly fire", shot and killed himself.

During September, there was an unsettling report that England and Scotland were "rotten with spies."

In the city of St. John's, deaths during September of 1914 included that of Mary Horwood, John Cormack and George Winslow, 84, who was better known as Sergeant Winslow.

An old British soldier who had served in the Crimean War, Winslow came to St. John's with his regiment in 1861. Eleven years later he joined the Newfoundland Constabulary as a drill instructor with the rank of sergeant.

On September 7, local newspapers reported that British casualties of war had reached 15,000.

On the same day, Newfoundland's Patriotic Fund reached $33,432.

During the fall of 1914, amidst news of deaths, marriages, cases of diphtheria, the poor state of the fishery, and the continuing serialized saga of the Mistress of Darracourt, The Evening Telegram carried lists of suggested war reading including such books as : How to Help Kitchener, The German Spy System and Germany's Swelled Head.

Appeals to patriotism were constant, as witness in A Woman's Recruiting Song, a poem by Paul A. Rubeens.

Oh we don't want to lose you.
But we think you ought to go,
For your King and your Country
Both need you so.
We shall want you and miss you.
But with all our might and main,
We will thank you, cheer you, kiss you
When you come back again.

Fred Wood of St. John's penned a poem bidding farewell to the boys who had already signed up:

Farewell farewell, gallant lads
Who sail across the sea
To battle in a neighbour's cause against the enemy.

On October 6, Holloway Studio had a set of 50 pictures of the Newfoundland Regiment's camp at Pleasantville up for sale.

On October 14, Garland's Bookstores had a Great War Sale and offered 20 per cent off selected items.

A column in The Evening Telegram titled The Latest from the Front reported the following items: Two German submarines had been destroyed during an attack on the Russian cruiser Pollada; The Turkish army numbered 900,000 men; The Germans had lost 20,000 men in battles in south Poland.

On October 15, well known Archbishop Michael Francis Howley died in St. John's.

The fourth of 13 children of Irish immigrants, Howley was born in St. John's in 1843. The first native born Newfoundlander to become a bishop and the first bishop of St. George's, Howley served on the west coast of Newfoundland for more than a decade before being transferred to St. John's. In 1904 he became Newfoundland's first archbishop. For twenty years, as bishop of St. John's, Howley worked to meet the social, religious and educational requirements of the day. He restored the cathedral, enlarged Littledale and St. Bonaventure's Colleges, and found time to write on many subjects. For ten years, he was a regular contributor to the Newfoundland Quarterly. Besides his Ecclesiastical History of Newfoundland published in 1888, he published a Book of Poems, which included the patriotic Fling out the Flag.

In 1898, Archbishop Howley, in co-operation with his brother, James, a geologist and author, gave the family home and property, Mount Cashel, to be used as a residence and industrial training place for orphaned boys, under the operation of the Irish Christian Brothers.

On October 16, The Evening Telegram reported the Newfoundland Regiment had arrived in Britain and all was well.

On October 24, the paper published an alphabetical list of all members of the Newfoundland Regiment who had left St. John's on board the Florizel.

Anthony James Stacey, number 466, was on the list, between James Snow, number 433, of St. John's, and Robert Sheppard, number 473, another St. John's man.

On October 26, it was reported Germany had lost 750,000 men, and that Canadian troops were now in Egypt.

That same day, the paper carried a poem called Somebody's Darling, contributed by Misses Mary and Loretta Hessian.

Into a world of the whitewashed halls,
Where the dead and dying lay
Wounded by bayonets, shells and balls
Somebody's darling was borne one day.
Somebody's darling so young and so brave,
Wearing yet on his pale sweet face,
Soon to be hidden by the dust of the grave,

The lingering light of his boyhood's grace.

The poem ended with a request:

Carve on the wooden slab at his head,
Somebody's darling slumbers here.

❋

The Florizel with the First 500 aboard lies at anchor in St. John's Harbour.
(courtesy The Fighting Newfoundlander)

 chapter seven

The First Five Hundred joined the Canadian contingent of 31 ships enroute to Great Britain on October 5, 1914. They reached Plymouth Sound in England on October 14.

It was October 3rd 1914, when we marched down to Harvey's wharf and boarded the S.S. Florizel, which was to be our home for the next sixteen days. Before going aboard we were issued kit bags and Canadian Army overcoats with their army buttons. This was about all we took on board. As the boat did not have the room or accommodation for so many people, hammocks had been rigged up in the hold for NCO's and other ranks, and on deck a cookhouse had been built and a stove installed. The Florizel was used as a passenger boat plying the run between St. John's, Halifax and New York. We were soon to find out that the water supply was getting low and we finished our trip drinking distilled water. That was the only time I remember when you could get froth on a glass of water just the same as you would on a glass of beer.

The first night aboard had its memories, some not pleasant, as we were anchored in St. John's harbor for twenty-four hours before sailing. It was before prohibition and everyone aboard was drinking to the health of every-

one else. My overcoat disappeared, or in other words, it was exchanged. Just before leaving, my brother Charlie gave me a valuable watch to take to England to be repaired. The watch was in my overcoat pocket. Later on, in Salisbury Plain, I retrieved the watch in the oddest fashion. There we had a Pte. Harrison Moore in our tent. On the day we arrived, he said, "Look what I found in my pocket!" Here was my brother's watch.

October 5th was a hazy day as we sailed out past the narrows. We did not know and could not see where we were going until we saw ships all around us. This was where we met the Canadian convoy of thirty thousand troops, the first one to set sail. There were three lines of ships, escorted by the British Navy. It was an impressive sight. One of the ships was the H.M.S. Magnificent. I will have something to say about her later on.

You must remember that in October 1914 there was a German squadron off the coast of Chile and although in pacific waters, chilling thoughts ran through our minds. In a sea battle on November 1st the British warships H.M.S. Good Hope, H.M.S. Monmouth and H.M.S. Glasgow were engaged. The H.M.S. Good Hope and H.M.S. Monmouth were sunk. It was the submarine that was the most dangerous at the time of our crossing the Atlantic. We, in the S.S. Florizel, being the last to join the convoy were in the rear and it seemed to us as if there was a forest of ships all around us. As it grew dark, we would see the flashing of signal lights from one ship to another. When you consider close to forty ships in three lines, the slowest ship was the fastest. It took us nine days to get to Plymouth, England.

The morning after leaving, while walking on the deck, Dr. Patterson called me and instructed me to report to Jack Robinson who was in charge of the Sergeant's mess. I was detailed to help wait on the Sergeants. This meant that I ate and slept in the saloon, which was comfort considering the rest were down in the hold in hammocks and eating "skilly" (a mixture of mutton and vegetables boiled up with black tea). I often took some of the leftovers from dinner to give some of my buddies a decent meal. I might mention that some good friends in St. John's had given us several barrels of apples for the boys. We had them all right, but paid for them, as the crew on the ship, the firemen, swiped and sold them to us.

There was a sense of humor sometimes at the expense of the unfortunate such as Rev Stenlake, who joined as a private and was not seen very often on deck as he was not very robust. After about seven days out at sea he managed to get on deck for parade with the Seventh Platoon. When Sylvester Madden (a wit) saw him coming he said, "here comes an apology of the graveyard."

We were very fortunate to make Plymouth our destination, without incident, as there were German warships on the high seas. It certainly was a welcome sight to see our warships and to hear the bands playing "O Canada". We were in the harbor six days before our turn arrived to go ashore.

The first five days at sea were spent organizing accommodations for the men on board.

The 3,000 tonne Florizel, built in 1909, had been specially constructed to contend with ice.

In addition to carrying passengers and freight on the St. John's, Halifax, New York run, she was engaged in the sea hunt every spring. Now, with more than 500 troops on board, it was necessary to improvise arrangements for sleeping, eating and sanitary facilities.

Everything worked out so well that at the end of the voyage Medical Officers Captain Lamont Paterson and Lieutenant Arthur Wakefield were able to report to the Governor that the men's health was excellent.

On October 12, two days before they arrived in England, the men held a concert on board the Florizel.

The concert was organized by Sergeant Owen Steele and the program which he put together comprised 25 items.

From Lance Corporal John Williams's opening solo "Anchored" through to Captain Bernard's repeat performance of La Marseillaise, every number drew enthusiastic applause.

The loudest applause was heard for renditions of "My Bonnie Lies Over The Ocean" and "Old Black Joe" sung by a group who dubbed themselves the "Florizel Glee Singers." [4]

**The order of the first Canadian Expeditionary Force
of which we sailed was:
Officers and Men 33,000 Landed at Plymouth October 14,1914.**

**SHIPS OF CONVOY
H.M.S MAJESTIC ***

H.M.S ECLIPSE	H.M.S. DIANA	H.M.S. CHARYBDIS (Flagship)
1. Megantic	12. Carribean	22. Tunisian
2. Ruthania	13. Athenia	23. Arcadian
3. Bermudian	14. Royal Edward	24. Zealand
4. Alaunia	15. Fraconia	25. Corinthian
5. Ivernia	16. Canada	26. Virginian
6. Scandinavian	17. Monmouth	27. Andania
7. Sicilian	18. Manitou	28. Saxonia
8. Montreal	19. Tyrolia	29. Grampian
9. Lapland	20. Scotian	30. Lakonia
10. Cassandra	21. Laurentic	31. Montezuma
11. Florizel		

H M S P R I N C E S S R O Y A L (left side)

H M S G L O R Y (right side)

Rear Cruiser: H.M.S. Talbot

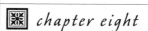 *chapter eight*

After disembarking in Devonport, England, the Newfoundland Regiment had a five hour train trip to reach Salisbury Plain, an area used for training British troops since the turn of the century. It would be their home for the next seven weeks.

The Newfoundlanders were assigned to the west side of the military area in Pond Farm Camp. They shared the area with the 4th Canadian Infantry Brigade and two Canadian cavalry units. Canadian headquarters were established at Bustard Camp, about three miles north of Stonehenge.

When war was declared in 1914, Colonel Sam Hughes, Canada's Minister of Militia and Defense, promised Great Britain 25,000 men. By September 8, a total of 32,665 Canadians had enlisted.

Canada's First Contingent, which arrived in England at the same time as the Newfoundland regiment, consisted of 30,621 men.

On Salisbury Plain, the turf that covered most of the 90 square miles of War Office Lands provided excellent training ground in dry weather. However, during the time the Newfoundlanders and Canadians were at Salisbury the weather was wet, cold and miserable.

In Britain that year, precipitation of 23.9 inches between mid-October and mid-February almost doubled the 32-year average. On some days, the rain was so heavy and the ground so muddy that training had to be cancelled. The unending rain was often accompanied by high winds which cut through the thin fabric of the unheated tents with bone chilling ferocity.

Here is Jim Stacey's recollection of that time:

Salisbury Plain

We then went to Salisbury Plain with the Canadians. Our camp was called "Pond Farm". We were put in our respective companies, seven to a tent. I was attached to the seventh Platoon, "B" Company. Lt. C.R. Ayre was in command. (When I went to England in 1961, I went to Salisbury Plain to find "Pond Farm" but without success. I found Bulford Camp and Lark Hill Camp and also took the opportunity to visit the monoliths at Stonehenge.

As October in England is usually a wet month, we were soon to find out that leather boots were no good to cope with the mud, so I bought a pair of knee rubbers at the canteen. Shortly thereafter, I put in for leave to go home to visit my parents at Benson, Oxford. Around the same time Sgt. Owen Steele, Orderly Sergeant, was required to go to the rail head at Bulford each day to get our rations. You can imagine the road conditions with all the rain, so Steele asked me for a loan of my knee rubbers and I wore his boots, which were about my size. The next day I received my pass for four days and away I went shod in Steele's boots.

The upshot was that it was fourteen days before I returned and in doing so got lost on the plains and stayed a night or so with the Canadian Regiment. Arriving back in camp and having overstayed my pass, Sgt. Major Bert Dicks had me, along with the rest of the defaulters, and there were many, up to the orderly room, where the Commanding Officer gave out his punishment. Being assigned to the Sergeant's mess, they were waiting for my help, so Dicks took me out and told me to go to work in the mess.

Sgt. Steele was very upset; he had only a week as orderly sergeant and had to wear my rubbers all the time as I was wearing his boots.

Every Regiment had a bugler and in some cases a bugle band (we had one later on). The bugler did all the calls such as: reveilles (wake up) fall in, cook house (to get your meals) and lights out or last post. The day I returned from leave, while passing through the Canadian lines, I heard a cacophony of sounds. The buglers generally went away from the regiment lines, to clumps of trees to practice. It seemed that every bugler was out practicing that day, as you could hear one continuous melody of different calls, echoing over hill and dell.

The first pay we received on the Plains was in gold, and that was the last, as gold became scarce. Speaking of money, I seemed to be never short. The eleven days I worked on the S.S. Florizel, I was paid one dollar per day by the owners, Harvey and Company, which to my mind was extra. I was as good as a passenger, having a good bed to sleep on in the lounge and the best kind of meals.

An incident happened at Salisbury Plain, which I did not understand until I read an article in the "Legionary". It happened about a week after our arrival there. All the units formed a hollow square and Lt. General E.A.H. Alderson, who was in command, told us we were going to have canteens. It did not interest me too much as beer never bothered me, but as I said the "Legionary" had an article about Sam Hughes who was a Boer War veteran and organized the first Canadian Contingent. It stated that he was a teeto-taler and did not allow canteens to the Canadians. This was so when we first arrived, but the situation here was different as there were English pubs in every village and these were where the troops went for refreshments. You can guess the rest. I remember after the canteens opened Pte. Joseph Good, an Englishman, who like myself, had joined up, often said he was going down for a "quiet pint", but on coming back it certainly did not seem that the pint of beer made him "quiet".

Sam Hughes, by the way, was also responsible for the introduction of the Ross rifle to the Canadians. We trained with them but did not use them in the field of battle. They could not stand up against war conditions. The Canadian soldiers used them, but exchanged them when they could for the short Lee Enfield. ✿

chapter nine

Early in December, orders came for the Newfoundland Regiment to leave Salisbury Plain.

On December 7, the men marched through deep mud past historic Stonehenge to Amesbury, where they boarded trains to Fort George in the Highlands of Scotland.

Fort George, which was to be their home for the next ten weeks, was a pleasant surprise after Salisbury Plain. All of A Company and some of B were given accommodation in buildings overlooking the main square of the fort, five men to a room. The remainder of B Company was housed in long, vaulted rooms built into the thick walls of the fort. Each room held 14 men.

Training was less rigorous than it had been at Salisbury Plain as the fort was observing winter hours of training. Reveille was at 7 a.m. and the first parade lasted from 9:15 a.m. to noon. After dinner there were two more hours of training.

A week after their arrival a local paper, the Inverness Courier, noted that the men of the Newfoundland Regiment were "well built, strapping fellows, full of vigor, hardy and strong."

When Christmas Day arrived, the men shared the contents of parcels from home, enjoyed an excellent dinner, and sang carols. A concert was held in the evening

Of the 13 soldiers who gave individual performances at the concert, six did not live to see Newfoundland again. For two of the soldiers, the Christmas at Fort George would be their last.

Private George Knight, who recited "The Face on the Barroom Floor" and Private John Dunphy, who sang the popular song "Stop That Talking" both died at Suvla Bay the following December. [5]

On New Year's Day, 1915, the Regiment enjoyed the hospitality of families in the nearby communities of Inverness, Ardersier and Nairn, but the day was saddened by the death of 20- year-old Private John Fielding Chaplin of B Company.

Chaplin died of an abdominal condition and was buried with full military honours in Ardersier Parish Churchyard. Jim mentioned his death in his memoirs:

Scotland

We could not stay on Salisbury Plain through the winter as we were not to be attached to the Canadians, so at the end of November, we boarded a train to go north. Passing through Basingstoke, a town where I remember spending a holiday in my school days with my Uncle Anthony Borlace. Basingstoke was a railway junction and he was station master with the G.W.R. We turned north up through the midlands and through the Black Country where the blast furnaces lit up the night sky with magnificent and colourful displays.

We arrived at last at our destination. Fort George, Inverness, a walled in fort, situated about twelve miles from the town of Inverness, would be our home for the winter. Inverness contained the barracks of and was the home of the Cameron Highlanders.

All of "A" Company and some of "B" Company were housed in buildings, and the remainder of "B" Company were housed in the stone fort itself. We stayed in the fort. The beds, which could be pulled out, consisted of three small mattresses that resembled a square biscuit. We therefore called them "biscuits". We spent Christmas and the New Year there and the Sergeant's Mess was still employing me.

Somehow, I could not get a pass to go on leave; they seemed to think I did not need one. All the rest of the battalion could get one when they wished. I had asked Sgt. Wilfrid Ayre, who was in charge of the mess, for leave, but could not get any satisfaction from him, so I planned to take it on my own. There was only one entrance to the fort and a guard was always on duty checking passes. In my case, it was different. There was a Sergeant outside the fort in charge of what was called the "Aeroplane Guard". This guard was assigned to the nearby seaplane base, and tasked to watch for any unusual

*activity. I had to take the Sergeant's meals to him, so I did not need a pass and
the guard on duty usually knew me. Just before the New Year, I took his sup-
per out to him. Since it was dark, instead of going back, I headed for the railway station in the village of Ardersier. I kept clear of the main road to the village, bought my ticket, boarded the train and waited for it to move, expecting at any moment for the Red Caps, the military police, to ask me for my
pass. If they asked for a pass, and you did not have one, it was just your hard
luck, as you would be arrested. Luck was my way. I spent the New Year in a
real Scottish way, (to my sorrow) as I landed in the barracks of the Cameron
Highlanders. I must have toasted too many "Burns". I was never so disgusted
in all my life. At least it taught me a lesson, which I never forgot.*

*After staying a week, I went back to face the music in the Sergeants' Mess.
The first person I saw was our Regimental Sergeant Major Paver. He asked
me where I was, and after telling him, I was fired from the mess, and told to
get my buttons polished and go on parade. That was something I had not done
since joining up in Newfoundland. I was back in the Seventh Platoon of "B"
Company with Lt. C.R. Ayre and Sgt. Kershaw. This particular morning
there was an inspection by the Commanding Officer, Lt. Col. R. de H.
Burton of "A" and "B" Companies. Everything went fine until the command
of "present arms", which I could not do. The CO noticed me fumbling and
Sgt. G. Byrne was told to take me aside and teach me how it was done. Being
in the ranks with the boys, I was to get the training that every soldier should
get: quick march, right turn and route marches, everything to make you hard
and fit. The fact remained; I was still in R.S.M. Paver's bad books and he had
to countersign all other ranks' passes. That is where he had it on me, but if I
could not get a pass I did the other thing, took French leave when needed.*

*Our first death in the Regiment occurred at Fort George on January 1,
1915, No. 484 Pte J.F. Chaplin. He was buried at Ardersier, but afterwards
transferred to the cemetery at Ayr. Ayr was also the headquarters of the Second
Battalion.*

In February, word came that the Newfoundland Regiment's C
Company, 250 strong, had sailed from St. John's on February 5. A and B
Companies were to meet them in Edinburgh.

The intention in Newfoundland had been to enlist an additional 250
men to meet a request for a 50 per cent reinforcement of the First 500.

However, when recruiting got underway again, so many able bodied
volunteers came forward that the Patriotic Association recommended
accepting enough recruits to bring the original Contingent up to full
British battalion size of 1,080 officers and men, together with a reserve
company of 250.

When two more drafts, D and E Companies, arrived in Scotland during March and May, the Regiment was brought up to slightly over battalion strength.

At the time of the First World War, the British Army fought in battalions, not regiments.

A battalion consisted of 992 soldiers and 30 officers subdivided into into four companies. Each company comprised four platoons, with four sections in every platoon. In this book we use the terms battalion and regiment interchangeably.

By the end of 1915, a total of 2,175 Newfoundlanders had been sworn into the Newfoundland Regiment, of whom 1,875 had gone overseas.

When A and B Companies arrived in Edinburgh, where they were to garrison the castle, they were greeted by the Pipes and Drums of the 4th Battalion, the Royal Scots Regiment, and paraded through the streets to Edinburgh Castle.

The men of the Newfoundland Regiment were the first colonial troops to be stationed in Edinburgh, and are still the only "non-Scottish" troops to have garrisoned Edinburgh Castle.

When Companies A and B met up with C Company, there was a spirited exchange of news from home. The seasoned veterans of A and B Company were anxious to hear all that had happened since they left Newfoundland four and a half months before.

Within a day, the Regiment was settled in quarters in barracks at Edinburgh Castle, high above the city.

While in Edinburgh, twelve members of the Regiment were appointed second lieutenants, all of them Blue Puttees. Of the twelve, half – Herbert Herder, Owen Steele, Richard Shortall, Rupert Bartlett, Fred Mellor, and Cecil Clift – would die in battle before the final year of the war.

On May 10, orders were given that the troops would be confined to barracks that evening, their last in Edinburgh. Determined to bid farewell to friends they'd met during their time in the city, a large number of the Newfoundland Regiment, including Jim Stacey, scaled the walls of the castle in what was dubbed "Operation Exodus."

With the coming of spring, we left Fort George, boarded a train at Ardersier and headed for Edinburgh. We were to be stationed at Edinburgh Castle. The march from the railway station to the castle with the Royal Scots band in the lead was one of the occasions which stands vividly in my memory. The road was a continuous rise in a circle and everything was aglow with light. We were now in a city for the first time. "C" Company was already here, when we arrived, and "D" Company arrived later, to bring the Battalion up to full strength. It was here that our physical instructor, Sgt. Major McKay, certainly put us through our exercises. We did not require a pass while stationed at the Castle. We could always go out after tea but had to be back by 11:00 p.m.

As summer approached there was talk of our leaving, and later this was confirmed. The last evening, orders were given that nobody was allowed out. It was unfortunate, as we had an invitation to visit a friend's house. We thought it a little too harsh, to be shut in for the last night. The only solution left was to get over the castle wall, which others and I did. How we got over the wall without mishap I do not know. I visited the castle in 1961 and looked down from the place where we scaled it. To me it seemed impossible; perhaps age dims the courage. We went to a gent's dress toilet room and cleaned ourselves up, and when we reached the street we saw everyone was let out. Perhaps our exploit was not in vain as the Commanding Officer had reversed his orders. My buddies and I fulfilled our engagement. The lady of the house said to us, "You know when I was walking along Princes Street, I saw several of your Regiment climbing over the castle wall." We said not a word.

While we were stationed in the castle, a German battle cruiser squadron attacked the North Sea ports (hit and run tactics). They seemed to have considerable success using their battle cruisers that were light, heavily armed and speedy. In this case, our battle cruisers caught up with them and sank the Blucher, which happened to be not as speedy as the rest. The officers that were taken prisoner were jailed in the castle. One died and the Newfoundland Regiment supplied the Guard of Honor at the funeral.

Another thing I remember while at the castle was being vaccinated. What an arm I had! I was off duty for over a month. From Edinburgh Castle we went by train to Hawick, then to Stobs Camp which is about two miles from Hawick on the Tweed. Here I made friends with a Mr. and Mrs. Robson. Mr. Robson was a Boer War veteran and now too old for the army. Since he could not serve, he and his wife thought the least they could do was to entertain those that were able. They were very kind to me, and even sent parcels to me when I was overseas. To repay them for their kindness, I sent them parcels of food during the Second World War. Here, as elsewhere, it seemed so easy for everyone to get a pass but me. R.S.M. Paver was in the way as he still had it in for me. I thought out a plan, as I wanted to go to my home that was in the south of England, a day's run in war times. I sent a letter to my younger brother, who was at home, and asked him to send a telegram to the effect that mother was sick and to come home at once. The telegram arrived and was passed to the CO. I received four days leave and my fare in the form of a ticket and pass for the journey. One day going and another returning, left me with only two days home which I did not think was enough, so I sent a letter back to the CO asking for four more days as mother had not improved. A week after my return Sgt. Major Dicks of "B" company told me with a smile on his face that he had received my letter that day. I do not know whether my letter was addressed correctly or not, but heard no more about it.

While we were on route marches, forming fours and all other kinds of stunts, trying to make good hard soldiers out of us, we had a light side, taking evenings down to Hawick. Stobs was neither a castle nor a fort, but a camp with tents. You were supposed to be in camp at "lights out", that is when the bugler sounded the last post. There were sentries around the whole camp and you could be sure that some of the boys would be arriving back after roll call.

In that case, you had to dodge the sentries and wait for your chance and make a run for your tent. There would be your sleeping space in the tent like a piece of pie, triangle shape. You had to get under your blanket in a hurry so the sentry could not find you. There were always some AWOL (absent without leave) and the regiment police would have a difficult job picking them up. There was one, picked up in Hawick selling coal in a cart, all dressed up minus his uniform and on his head, he wore a bowler hat.

While here, the Newfoundland Colours were presented to the Regiment by Lady MacGregor, wife of a former Governor. Sir William MacGregor, held office from 1904 to 1909. It was a colourful ceremony. ✵

John Shiwak of Labrador during training in Scotland
(courtesy The Trail of the Caribou)

 chapter ten

On May 11, 1915, the Newfoundland Regiment moved from Edinburgh to Stobs, 50 miles away. At Stobs Camp, Companies A, B, C, D and E were joined in July by another draft, F Company, bringing the regiment up to a strength of 1,500.

Dr. Wilfred Grenfell of St. Anthony, on Newfoundland's northern peninsula, was responsible for the formation of F Company.

Born in the English village of Parkgate in 1865, Grenfell first came to Newfoundland in 1892 as a combination physican/ missionary with the newly formed Mission to Deep Sea Fishermen.

In his book, Forty Years for Labrador, Grenfell said what greeted him on his arrival in St. John's was "dense columns of smoke ... for the third time in its history the whole city of St. John's was in flames."

The Great Fire of 1892 ruined three fourths of the city of St. John's; $20 million worth of property, some 2,000 houses and stores, were destroyed; and 11,000 people were left homeless.

Grenfell stayed briefly in the still smoldering city then sailed on the Albert to Labrador, where he visited the five stations of the Moravian missionaries.

In 1893, Grenfell established a hospital in Battle Harbour, the first on the Labrador coast. During the winter of 1899-1900, he set up his medical quarters in St. Anthony, in 1912, he formed the International Grenfell Association. By 1914, the organization had established four hospitals and six nursing stations on the Labrador coast.

In March of 1915, from his base in St. Anthony, Grenfell offered to raise and drill a small company which would maintain its own identity upon reaching the capital city of St. John's.

Among this reserve force was John Shiwak, an Inuit from Rigolet.

Shiwak enlisted in the Regiment on July 1, 1915, and went to France as part of a reinforcement draft after the July 1 decimation of the Regiment at Beaumont Hamel.

Posted with C Company, Shiwak quickly gained a reputation as the "premier sniper" of the Regiment, but his competence with a rifle wasn't enough to bring him safely home

The young man from Labrador was killed on November 21, 1917, during the second day of the battle of Cambrai, when a German shell exploded amongst a column of soldiers, killing him and six others.

When Grenfell's F Company arrived at Stobs Camp John Shiwak and other members of the Newfoundland Regiment, including Jim Stacey, were kept busy with rigorous training.

In August, orders came that Regimental Headquarters and the four senior Companies would move to Aldershot on August 2. Everyone else would stay in Ayr. Jim Stacey was among those sent to Aldershot:

About the middle of July we packed up for another move. This time we headed for the south of England, Aldershot. When we arrived, we were billeted in the Badajoz barracks. We knew that this was the last stop before going into the theatre of war. The horse transport was formed and we picked up, the last, of what was needed. We turned in our Ross rifles and received the short Lee Enfield 303, with sharpened bayonets, in their place. The Lee Enfield was the standard rifle used by the British Army. We were now getting ready for active service. General Kitchener and King George V reviewed us. As we, the first Battalion, had signed on for only twelve months, we were now asked to sign on for the duration of the war and most of us did so.

It was no trouble now to get a pass for leave, for a short while. All you had to do was to get a blank pass, fill it in and hand it to the Regimental Sergeant Major, who of course was Paver (who would not sign a pass for me) and then the CO would countersign it. Thinking this would be the last chance for leave I filled in a pass and forged the CO's name and thought it would pass the Red Caps. It was not good enough so I landed in the clink. I was taken before the CO and given seven days CB, meaning confined to barracks and was required to report to the Orderly Officer every half-hour. I thought, for the moment, that my plans to go home before going to the front were off, until I went to my barracks to find one of my room mates there; all the rest had gone on leave. He said to me, "this is a bad state of affairs". "Why is that?" I asked. "I have a pass", says he, "but I have no money and can't use it". He had a rail ticket to London with the pass. I asked him how much he wanted for it and he asked for half a crown. This amount, I gave him and I was the owner of the pass and the ticket. His name was mine now and the Military Police did not know that it was not. It was now safe to go to London which I did, and from there I went home and took ten days leave. I figured it was just as well to get killed for a sheep as for a lamb. When I returned, low and behold, the Regiment had gone overseas and I was left behind with a few stragglers with nothing to do and no one to look after me for a while. I thought that was trouble enough, so I had to be careful. My home was only thirty miles from Aldershot I hit on a plan to make another trip home. Mon Noseworthy and I hired bicycles and left after dark. Our hunger was satisfied by swiping apples, which were just ripe for eating, from an orchard on the way home. We were afraid to stay too long so we rode back the next day. We did not hear a word about all this though it was a serious offence. I never laid eyes on Sergeant Major Paver afterwards. He was only at Suvla Bay a few days when he became sick and the next thing we heard he was back with the Second Battalion at Ayr where he stayed to the end.

Those now left behind at Aldershot were all collected together and sent to Ayr to form the second Battalion. There we were billeted in Newtown Park School. A coincidence occurred in New York, when I visited my son (George) in 1957. I was introduced to the wife of a Newfoundland soldier of World War II. She was Scots and from Ayr. When I told her that I was at Ayr and stayed a short while in Newtown Park School, she told me that was where she went to school.

We received reinforcements at Ayr. After signing on again, to be on hand to finish the war (this was the third time), we, the first draft, boarded a train for Liverpool on November 17, 1915 (my birthday). From there we boarded the S.S. Olympic, a troop ship of fifty thousand tons. It must have had on board, reinforcements for every unit in the Near East, Salonika and Gallipoli. Although it was an uneventful voyage we had an escort of destroyers. There were five thousand troops aboard and it was a good thing we did not meet any trouble for we were as far down in the hold as we could possibly be. They called it H deck that was eight decks below. One of the bulkhead watertight compartments was always closed. If one was down below and wanted to go to the other side of the ship it would take half an hour to do so. There was a brass plate on the main deck; it read, "If you walked three and one half times around, you completed a mile".

In August, when 1,076 men of the Newfoundland Regiment left England for Gallipoli, the members of E and F Company, soon to be joined by G and the first draft of H, were moved to Ayr, Scotland, to establish the depot and training and enforcement centre and form a Regimental band.

There was hope of raising a second active battalion, but it was soon realized that Newfoundland would be hard pressed to maintain a constant flow of reserves for one fighting battalion when it became involved in the battle on the Western Front.

The designation of the new formation was given as the 2nd (Reserve) Battalion and its main function was to provide trained and equipped drafts of reinforcements for the 1st Battalion

Later, two reserve Companies were sent from Newfoundland with the designation A and B Companies, 3rd Battalion. The last full company to proceed overseas in 1915 as a single draft was G Company which arrived in Britain on November 9.

In October, the officer commanding the depot in Ayr reported that the departure of 104 men to reinforce the 1st Battalion in Gallipoli had left him so short of men he felt there would be difficulty in providing further drafts to keep the battalion at full strength.

His recommendation that future reinforcements be sent in batches of 100 as soon as they were available, whether trained or untrained, was adopted by the Reserve Force Committee.

The final draft of the year, consisting of 100 men as an initial installment of H Company, left Newfoundland in December. They arrived in Ayr on January 4 and were added to the strength of G Company.

It was in Ayr, birthplace of Scottish poet, Robert Burns, and the place that would be the Regimental depot for most of the war, that the Newfoundland Regiment acquired its famous mascot, Sable Chief, a magnificent Newfoundland dog, presented to the 2nd Battalion by a Canadian officer serving in England. [8] ⊛

Private Frank Lind who went missing in France
July 1, 1916 (courtesy The Trail of the Caribou)

🔳 *chapter eleven*

Frank Lind from Betts Cove, Notre Dame Bay, arrived in Aldershot in August.

At age 35, he was considerably older than most of the others in the Regiment. In 1894, he had been working for the Fogo firm of J. W. Hodge. He later worked for Ayre & Sons in St. John's, but was back in Fogo and working as a clerk when war broke out. Lind enlisted in the Newfoundland Regiment as a private and was sent to Scotland in February 1915.

After going overseas, he began a regular correspondence with the Daily News in St. John's. Within a very short time, his chatty letters, keeping the folks at home abreast of what was happening to their boys overseas, became one of the most popular features in the paper.

In May 1915, in a letter written from Scotland, Lind mentioned it was impossible to get good tobacco overseas and expressed his longing for a May-o-lind, a square pound of Mayo brand tobacco costing 40 cents.

Within days of the letter appearing in the paper, donations of tobacco began pouring in.

Soon afterwards, the Daily News, the government of Newfoundland, and the St. John's based Imperial Tobacco Company established a fund to provide for tobacco and cigarettes for the boys overseas.

When the tobacco and cigarettes were delivered – each parcel was separately packed and contained a May-o-Lind as well as five packs of Gem cigarettes – Lind was immediately dubbed Mayo Lind. The nickname stuck. In 1919, Robinson & Company published a collection of his letters to the Daily News in a book titled *The Letters of Mayo Lind.* Robinson Blackmore re-published the book in 2001.

Shortly after arriving in Aldershot, Lind said the town less than 40 miles from London was a temporary home to about 250,000 soldiers. *"The town is up to date,"* he told his readers in Newfoundland, *"and a man can buy anything from a uniform button to a horse and cab."* [9]

On August 13, Lind reported that Lord Kitchener, the Secretary of War, had visited Aldershot and left the Newfoundlanders in no doubt as to where their next move would be. *"I'm sending you to the Dardanelles shortly, so be prepared, for when the order comes for it will come sharply,"* he wrote, quoting Kitchener.

Following Kitchener's address, Lind said the Regiment was lectured by medical officer Wakefield on use of a gas helmet.

As well, he said, a Mr. Kieley of the Nickel Theater in St. John's was on hand with a "moving picture machine" to film the Regiment for the people home in Newfoundland.

On August 17, when King George V visited the Regiment at Aldershot, the men knew the Royal inspection had only one meaning. They were about to be sent to the Front.

On the morning of August 20, 1915, the 1st Newfoundland Battalion embarked at Devonport, where the First 500 had landed 10 months earlier.

It was a beautiful day when the Newfoundlanders, numbering 34 officers and 1,042 other ranks, boarded the transport ship, Megantic, enroute to Gallipoli, where they were to join the 29th Division in Suvla Bay on the Gallipoli Peninsula.

As noted earlier, the British at this time fought by battalions, not by regiments.

A battalion was 1,022 men, subdivided into four companies and further subdivided into four platoons. A brigade was made up of four battalions. Three brigades made up a division.

The 29th Division consisted of the 86th, 87th, and 88th Brigade.

The 88th Brigade was comprised of four battalions: The 4th Worcestershire Regiment, 2nd Hampshire Regiment, 1st Essex Regiment and the Newfoundland 1st Battalion.

Enroute to Gallipoli, widely reputed to be a hell hole where the average length of a soldier's life was just three weeks, the first stop was Malta.

Then it was on to the land locked harbor of Mudros, on the island of Limnos, where the harbour was jammed with ships: warships, troop transports, hospital ships.

Busy, bustling Mudros was the base of Allied operations in the eastern Mediterranean. The Gallipoli Peninsula was only 50 miles away.

Much to their surprise, the Newfoundlanders didn't land in Mudros.

Acting on new orders, the Megantic continued on to Alexandria where the Newfoundland Regiment arrived on September 1. They immediately took trains to Cairo, a night journey of 130 miles up the Nile valley.

In Cairo, the Newfoundlanders were housed in the Abbassia Barracks, where they had to sleep on the stone floors as there was no furniture whatsoever. After four days, the men moved to tents in Polygon Camp, two miles away, where they stayed for a further 10 days.

It was in Cairo, which Frank Lind described as one of the most interesting cities in the world, that the Newfoundlanders first met and became friends with troops from Australia and New Zealand, the Anzacs.

On September 18, the Newfoundland Regiment departed Alexandria enroute to Mudros. The following day, they boarded the coastal steamer, Prince Abbas, for the six-hour trip to Suvla Bay.

On arrival at what was known as Kangaroo Beach, a lighter, a motor driven flat bottomed boat with a steel plated deck and sides capable of carrying as many as 500 men or 50 horses, brought them ashore.

The Newfoundlanders arrived in Suvla Bay in the middle of the night.

By 8 a.m. they were undergoing heavy shelling from Turkish batteries situated on hills enclosing three sides of rocky Suvla Plain. The shelling resulted in 16 members of the Regiment being wounded. Among them was Battalion Adjunct Captain Walter Rendell, who was evacuated to Mudros that afternoon. It would be a year before he rejoined the Regiment on the Western Front. Rendell's place as Adjunct was taken by Captain Arthur Raley.

In Suvla Bay, the Newfoundlanders were quickly introduced to trench warfare. Ten days after landing they were placed on front line duty within 50 yards of the Turkish position.

The Newfoundlanders were not called upon to launch an attack on the Turks; they spent their days in the trenches keeping an eye on the enemy, dodging enemy snipers, maintaining the trenches and cheering as they observed the British Navy shelling the Turks.

Part of every day's routine involved "picking shirts,"[10] an attempt to get rid of the lice which thrived in the unsanitary environment in which the men existed.

It was in Suvla Bay that the Newfoundland Regiment had its first casualties in action.

On September 22, Private Hugh McWhirter, age 21, was killed by a Turkish shell.

Excerpt of poem
WHO WILL WEEP FOR HUGH MCWHIRTER?
by Paul O'Neill

Private Hugh McWhirter
is now mocked by weeds
'though he is handsome,
boyish, just turned twenty-one.
He's been like that
since August twenty-second
nineteen hundred and fifteen.
He was the first to die
from Newfoundland.

He may perhaps have seen
the name Gallipoli
on some school map
of Turkey or The Darandelles
but thought no more
than if had been
Samarkand or Timbuktu,
but now he's linked to it
for all eternity
by acts of Englishmen
he never knew.

He fell-
one autumn morning
that was out of tune with time,
and sand
as thick as snows of home
became the yellow of his hair,
His warm blood drained away
on spears of others hates.

Who weeps for Hugh McWhirter now?

The following day, Private William Hardy was hit and killed by a sniper's bullet.

Both men were buried on the slopes of Hill 10 overlooking the bay, in a cemetery that contains eight of the 43 graves of Newfoundlanders killed in Suvla Bay.

On September 27, in one of his regular letters to the Daily News, Frank Lind said,

Tell all at home that we are doing our best to bring honour to Newfoundland and they need not be ashamed of the Newfoundland Regiment. [11]

On October 30, he expressed sympathy for captured Turkish prisoners and said the Turks were far cleaner fighters than the Germans.

The Germans chain Turks on to the guns so they cannot retreat even if they want to. The Turks never use gas and have been known to carry men of the British side back to the British lines after dressing their wounds. [12]

Early in November, the job of clearing out a Turkish sniper's nest concealed on a slope was given to members of the Newfoundland Regiment. Their success in capturing the hill led to it becoming known as Caribou Hill in honour of the Caribou Regiment. [13]

The action on Caribou Hill won a Military Cross for the Newfoundland Regiment's Lieutenant James Donnelly, and a Distinguished Conduct Medal for Sergeant Walter Green of Avondale and Private Richard Hynes of Fogo. Lance Corporal Fred Snow of St. John's received a Military Medal.

Later in the Gallipoli campaign, Private William Gladney of Bell Island was awarded a Distinguished Conduct Medal for locating four machine guns, shooting two Turkish sentries and returning to his line with valuable intelligence information. [14]

John Gallishaw, who was a student at Harvard University when he left to join the Newfoundland Regiment, was among the Newfoundlanders who served in Suvla Bay.

In his 1917 book, Trenching at Gallipoli, he provided a first person account of his time there beginning with time spent in the camp in Cairo where the men rode donkeys across the desert in order to catch the street car that ran into the city. He said every afternoon as soon as dinner was over little native boys pestered the men to hire donkeys. These were the same boys who poked their heads into the mens' tent each morning and implored them to buy a newspaper. On page 30, Gallishaw noted no one needed reveille in Egypt.

The thing that woke us was a native yelling "Eengaleesh paper, veera good; veera good, veera nice; fifty thousand Enengaleesh killed in the Dardanelle; veera good, veera nice."

In Suvla Bay, he told how the men ate their meals "such as they were" in the dugouts, to the accompaniment of "Turkish Delight," the Newfoundlanders name for shrapnel. Early morning tea was referred to as "gunfire." Bully beef, biscuits and jam were dietary staples. The drinking water had to be boiled and was so flat and tasteless that once a week the men were given a spoonful of lime juice to add to their water bottles. Twice a week, said Gallishaw, on what the men referred to as Rum Days, there was a special treat.

An officer carrying a large stone jar bearing the magic letter in black paint, P.D.R., Pure Demerara Rum. This he doled out as if every drop had cost a million dollars. Each man received just enough to cover the bottom of his canteen, not more than an eighth of a tumbler. [15]

According to Gallishaw, sickness and snipers' bullets resulted in the death of 30 men every day. He said those who were wounded were looked upon as lucky. The best thing wished a man was a "cushy wound" that would not prove fatal, or a "Blighty one" that would get him invalided back to England.

The men called corporals and sergeants Jack, Bill or Mac. A Turk was a Turkey, Abdul Pasha or a cigarette maker. A man shot through the head was said to have "lost his can." A dead man was called a "washout" or it was said to have "copped it." The caution to keep your head down was always stated as: Keep your napper down low. To get wounded by one of their own, so called friendly fire, was to get "a dose of three-o-three," as the bullet had a diameter of three hundred and three thousandths of an inch.

Frank Lind was nearby the day Gallishaw was shot in the back by a Turkish sniper.

He told his Daily News readers that Gallishaw, whom he described as a young man always in a good humor, said "That's a darn good shot whoever shot it" as he fell to the ground.

He wrote too that Gallishaw's motto was: "Ah, what odds, it might be worse." [16]

When he was invalided out of Gallipoli, Gallishaw was taken first to Alexandra where he stayed for six weeks, and then on to Wandsworth Hospital in London, England.

In hospital in London, he met up with an Australian soldier he'd first encountered in Suvla Bay. During the course of one of their conversations a curious Gallishaw inquired as to why the dark haired Australian was called "White George."

His real name was George White, explained the Aussie, which appeared on the regimental as White, George, hence the nickname.

In Suvla Bay, hot weather brought plagues of flies bearing diseases which caused even more casualties than Turkish shells and bullets.

For veterans of the Newfoundland Regiment who served in Gallipoli, however, the memory of everything else that happened in that campaign was overshadowed by memories of what was always called the November Storm, or the Big Flood.

This ordeal inflicted more than 5,000 casualties on the Allied Forces in the Suvla area alone.

During the first three weeks of November, a series of gales destroyed shipping and seriously damaged beach installations from Cape Helles to Suvla. The fiercest gale of all was the one which started on November 26, blowing first from the southwest, then veering to the north and bringing rapidly dropping temperatures. The electrical storm which accompanied the wind and rain lasted for four hours in the Suvla area.

The troops were drenched and worse was yet to come.

The section of trenches being held by the Newfoundland Regiment was at the lowest point of the front line. With other trenches forming natural drainage ditches, a torrent of water flowed down into the Newfoundland position, flooding the trenches and carrying with it blankets, equipment, rifles and the bodies of drowned men.

Before nightfall, an icy hurricane was sweeping down the length of the Gallipoli Peninsula. The sleet turned to snow and temperatures dropped well below freezing. By the morning of the 28th the water in many of the flooded trenches was topped by ice half an inch thick. The frost continued for two more days. It was the worst weather the Peninsula had seen in 40 years.

Many of those who escaped drowning suffered severe frostbite and trench foot, brought on by continual standing in cold water. This painful condition, if not checked, soon led to gangrene and possible amputation.

As a result of the storm, 150 Newfoundlanders were sent to the hospital ships for medical treatment.

John Gallishaw wasn't in Suvla Bay for the Big Flood, but from his hospital bed in Alexandra, he heard survivors saying as they lay on the beach waiting to be taken to hospital ships they saw the bodies of at least 2,000 men who had frozen to death.

Frank Lind ended up in Floriana Hospital in Malta after the Big Flood. From hospital, he once again expressed his sympathy for the Turks. *Poor Mr. Turk had it worse than we ...and 100s were drowned.*

Lind told his Daily News readers that when he first arrived in Gallipoli his platoon contained 68 men, only one of whom was still fit for duty.

A withdrawal from Suvla had come under consideration in late

September.

On November 23, Britain's War Committee ruled in favour of total evacuation of the Gallipoli Peninsula. Evacuation of the Newfoundland Regiment began on December 18.

On December 19, troops left at Suvla and Anzac made every effort to deceive the Turks by pretending to carry on with normal activity.

In The Fighting Newfoundland, Nicholson offers the following description of preparing an unmanned rifle for firing as given by Captain George Hicks.

Suspended from the trigger of a rifle that had been wired in position was a tin can partially filled with sand. Above it was another can filled with water, which very slowly leaked into the can below. When the combined weight of the sand and water in the lower can amounted to about seven pounds, the trigger would be pulled and the rifle discharged.

Early on the morning of December 20, the majority of the Newfoundland troops were withdrawn to the island of Imbros, 15 miles from the Gallopoli peninsula. The rest, consisting mostly of A and B Company, were taken to Mudros.

In what seemed an impossible feat, 83,000 men, 186 guns, nearly 1,000 vehicles, and 4,700 mules and horses had been safely evacuated from Anzac and Suvla.

In late December, the 1st Newfoundland Battalion, with the 29th Division, landed at Cape Helles to reinforce and assist in the withdrawal from that front.

Jim Stacey arrived in Mudros in late November.

We arrived at Mudros Bay, Island of Lemnos, on November 26th. We were delayed going to Suvla Bay because of a storm on the 27th. While here, we were paid ten shillings, by Lt. P. Bartlett, which we did not need, as there was no place to spend it. Lighters took us to Suvla Bay on the night of December 1st. That same night we took our positions on the front line. The storm that delayed our landing was terrible; it washed out the trenches and then froze. There were quite a few of the Royal Scots Regiment frozen to death and many of our boys had "trench feet", which meant feet swollen from being exposed to so much water. The big problem at Suvla was getting water to drink. Some came in petrol tins with a bad taste of gasoline in it and the well where we first obtained good water turned into mud water. This is the kind of water our cooks used for cooking and tea making. When eating stew, you would be cracking grit with your teeth.

This was the beginning of my active service. There was not much shelling but small arms (303) after dark; both sides kept up a continuous barrage. Stray bullets and sniper-fire caused most of our casualties. We would fire over the parapet at night but not at any particular target. When darkness came we would move around in the open bringing up rations, etc. We had to get used to the mole life; we did not dare show our heads, as the Turk snipers were good shots. There was a lot of sickness caused by bad water, dysentery and yellow jaundice. It was a sorry sight to see the sick men leaving the line to go down to the beach (at the most only three miles away) to the cleaning station and having to take their full equipment with them. They would go a few yards and have to rest.

I had not been there long before being detailed for the "Listening Post", which was just outside the angle where the trench took a turn. Six of us had to crawl out through a hole in our barbed wire to a distant place, lie down, listen, wait, look to see if the enemy was on the prowl and give the alarm. If they attacked, you would be sacrificed. We had orders to use our firearms only in an emergency. Our bayonets were attached to our puttees. Of course, this post was only used at night. It was close to where the bombers had an over-sized catapult on the front line, which threw homemade bombs made out of tin cans, which had a slow fuse. Outside listening we would hear the creaking noise caused by the catapult being wound up by hand to stretch the elastic. We would know what to expect when we would see a bomb coming overhead and falling to our left with sparks flying not very far away from us. At the same time, the Turks would put a barrage of fire right along the line. As we lay as close to the ground as possible, the bullets passing over our heads deafened us. I will leave it to you to pass judgment on what was said, about the bombs, by the listening patrol to Lt. Jack Clift and Sgt. Paddy Byrne who were in charge of the first bomb squad. A stray bullet had killed Capt. Charles Wighton a few days before.

This duty was not too bad, when you got used to it, as the rest of the day you were off duty and would have a good sleep, that is, if you could. When you wrapped yourself in the blanket and got warm and comfortable your bosom friends, the fleas, started to enjoy themselves. It was an everlasting job in trying to combat them as the ground was full of them. Every day you had to pick your shirt. One plan was to turn the shirt inside out; that would fool them for a while but they would soon get around to the other side again. There were very strict orders with regard to cleanliness because of the fleas. If one threw an empty bully beef tin on the parapet, the punishment was that you had to go up and get it in daylight with a chance that a sniper would get you.

Anyone could see that we in Suvla Bay would not have a ghost of a chance if the Turks had modern weapons. It was only three miles from the beach to the front line trench. When Bulgaria went over to the enemy, the Germans could ship modern arms to Turkey, so the top brass thought it was best to get out. The rumours started to circulate that evacuation was in the wind. We had to get off without the Turks knowing about it, which seemed impossible. We had to bluff our way in order to have the Turks believe we were going to attack. The last line of defense was prepared on the beach. The best and strongest were picked to go to the beach and build this line (there were not too many). We left for the beach with our full equipment, a shovel and extra fifty rounds of ammunition. It wasn't easy trying to squeeze down through the communications trenches, as they were not built for such loads. Lt. Owen Steele was in charge. It turned out to be a fine place with lots of food. The Turks were on the hills three miles away and could see every movement on the beach. The plan started two weeks before the final get off. We kept up continuous rifle fire through the night. It would begin about dark, from 6 to 7 p.m. we would keep firing, from 7 to 8 p.m. We would not fire a shot, then from 8 to 9 p.m. we would fire again and go until dawn.

The next week it would be the reverse. This was to put the Turks off guard. If there were a time when no shots were fired from the beach the Turks would know that something was up. There was one battery (three guns) left until the last when the guns were shifted from one emplacement to another. They were shifted finally to the Red Cross clearing station, where there were tents and one man was left to keep the candles burning. Inside the line, on the beach there was a pile of bully beef boxes, etc. They were all empty and to this pile more and more were added. Just about sundown a boat would show itself around the head of the bay, which would make the Turks think that reinforcements were arriving instead of leaving. What interested me most was the warship in the bay, firing broadside at the Turks' line upon the hills. We could easily see as the shells struck amid a lot of smoke, noise, dust and flying rock. We would then watch the return fire. We could see the shells dropping with a splash around the ship. When the splashes got nearer, the warship would move off to put them off their mark and then would blast the hills again.

No shells came near us all the time we were there even though we were between the fire. As time went on, there were less and less in the lines and the final night about thirty volunteers were left in the front line. This is how the ceasefire paid off: the Engineers planted "trip bombs" in and around the trenches so that there would be some explosions after everyone had left; they used biscuit tins in which were placed lit candles and fuses cut to different lengths attached to bombs. When the bombs exploded, it gave the impression that we were carrying on as usual. This gave those that remained time to get to the beach.

Lighters were on the beach to take us to the warship in the bay, which happened to be the H.M.S. Magnificent. This ship was one of our escorts when we landed at Plymouth in October 1914. We were certainly jammed aboard as we had our full kits on our backs. The sailors tended to our needs and looked after us. As we got settled down, someone said, "get up and see the supply dump go up". I had enough for that day, December 20, 1915, and said, "to hell with the dump". In 1961 at his home near Seven Oaks in Kent, England, I was talking with Lt. Col. Hadow, who was our Commanding Officer at the time. He said he remembered in his early days that the H.M.S. Magnificent was a battleship of the first line. She seemed quite small to me.

Rumours were around that we were going back to England. They were still on the go after we landed on the Grecian Island of Imbros. The Island is about half way between the Gallipoli peninsula and the island of Lemnos. There we stayed for two days rest. We boarded lighters that brought us back to where we came from only further up the coast to Cape Helles, W Beach.

Below are some verses of a song composed by the Dardanelles Companies at this particular time:

In the night they let us wander
There was no one sent to meet
Till we found some empty dugouts
Where to rest our weary feet.
Airplanes dropped bombs upon us
Shells went screeching overhead
Shelter from the rain was asked for
"There is none" the staff all said.
Then the order came to dress up
To get picks and shovels from Headquarters
They brought back no bloody shovels
And I fear the story is true
For they raided and stole puddings
Pinched the General's turkey, too.
And for Christmas cheer they gave us
Bully beef and biscuits few
No tobacco, rum or pudding
Did we grumble - wouldn't you?
All our lousy shirts and jam tins
O'er the parapet did throw
Did the staff complain about it?
No! They chucked it long ago.
Capt. Wilson says we are dirty
Armstrong's views are just the same
So we are never downhearted
What is dirt compared to fame?

Our landing area was close to where the S.S. River Clyde went aground when the Twenty-ninth Division first landed; now she was used as a wharf. From here we went ashore and went to work for the final evacuation. We were billeted where the Greeks had been employed, chopping wood for the fires so the bakers could bake their bread. Now that they were gone, we were employed to do the same thing; the fires were kept burning but there was no bread baked. It was only a bluff to fool the Turks. Other parties were fixing up a trench for a last ditch stand and building bridges. All the transport on Gallipoli was assigned to the Indians. Our own transport was left in Egypt. It was at Cape Helles, where we came in contact with the Indian transport. It was interesting to watch the way they prepared their noon meal, which consisted of rice. I was wondering what one of them was going to do, when he took his turban off his head and started to unwind it, took up one corner on which was a knot, untied it and spread its contents over the rice. The watch I had was gunmetal, which I had bought before leaving Newfoundland. The novelty was that it had an alarm and could be set like a clock. The time part was out of order, but the alarm was working perfectly and would make a buzzing sound. Some of the Indians were interested in anything that was bright such as rings, watches and knives. One of them became interested in my watch, so to interest him more I set the alarm going. He wanted to buy it. The upshot was he gave me ten shillings and another watch and chain for it.

The ships or lighters came close to the beach. We had a job to help load them with stores. It was not a very healthy place as the Turks could infiltrate from Suvla Bay, from where we had just left. All along the beach the rising banks of sand were terraced with dugouts. In the back we were sheltered from the front line fire but not from Suvla Bay, so the Turks could get a direct hit on the terraced dugouts. Occasionally, we would hear the shells come whistling through the air and we looked to see where they would strike. Sometimes one would land among us on the beach. You could develop a sense of knowing by the report of the gun if it was coming your way. It was no laughing matter, but what made it seem so funny was that the shell would strike the dugout amid smoke and dust, caused by the shell exploding. You would think that the occupants were finished, then as the smoke drifted away everything would be still.

Suddenly it would come to life and the inmates would get up and start to run in all directions.

Cape Helles is the nearest point across the Dardanelles to Asia. The Turks had a gun that we called "Asiatic Annie". It would take thirty seconds from when you heard the report for a shell to land on W Beach. The French had a bugler there to give the warning to get under cover. There would be quite a scramble when the warning came. The Indian transport would stay put with dire consequences. They would never leave their seats; even if they got bogged down in the mud, you had to pull them, their mules and Transport out of it.

Now there was more trouble, the liquor stores were disappearing. You could see what was happening, so the order came to smash every bottle that could be found.

I noticed on the beach some old cannon balls crated up with Sir Ian Hamilton's home address on them. I need not wonder if he received them because we were lucky to get off ourselves. The cannon balls, no doubt, came from the old fort of Sedd-el-Rhar, which was close by. Now it had reached a stage when you could help yourself to anything in the Ordnance Stores, which I did, only to lose it all at kit inspection at Suez (except one hundred packages of Flag cigarettes). I was looking around and saw a Newfoundland guard pro-

tecting some crates. There was quite a queue, so I fell in line with the rest. They were handing out boxes of Flags of five hundred cigarettes. I managed to get two boxes, which just fitted in the pack that held my overcoat and blankets. They were afterwards a lifesaver, as you will learn later on.

While we were working, a party was sent to Brigade Headquarters to procure picks and shovels. They were delayed so they looked around to see what they could take with them. They found some Christmas puddings and turkeys. You know the rest. Only one person was caught with the goods and that was Jelico Walsh (now Dr Walsh). He was put in the guard tent where he stayed until we reached Suez. After a while he was let off.

The evening of January 8th, the day before the final evacuation, we were having our last meal sitting around the fire just outside the dugouts, which were terraced on the sandbank and built mostly of sandbags. Shell infiltrated from Suvla, struck the dugout just above ours and landed right in the centre of the fire. Sgt. C. Garland was sitting on the outside and the percussion before the shell burst overbalanced him. He turned a somersault and as he was falling, he received a wound in the back. There were two others wounded and Pte Robert Morris was killed. He was the last Newfoundlander to be buried on the Dardanelles and I helped with the stretcher that took him to the grave already dug.

We moved out, right after this incident, passing the beached S.S. River Clyde to a lighter on the other side, where we boarded a ship that took us to Alexandria, Egypt. There we stayed aboard for the night. That closed the chapter to that operation of folly. There was no medal struck or the like given to anyone.

No rank, except officers, were allowed ashore that night. Some of us thought we should be, so we slid down a rope on the shore side and went ashore. Having had a look at the town, we arrived back in time (broke), but unfortunately some were caught. I was not.

It was very interesting to see the natives, grown men, scrambling for a few pennies we had tossed over the side of the boat. The next day we boarded a train that took us to Suez. On our way we stopped at a station to stretch our legs. There were hawkers selling oranges for a penny each and very few of us had any money. For their safety the hawkers had the oranges in small brin bags (burlap sandbags). These were tucked under their arms with the mouth held tightly. You had to give them the money before you saw an orange. Most of us had not seen an orange for six months. While an intended buyer attracted hawker's attention, another was behind with his jack knife slitting up the bag. Of course, the oranges disappeared in a hurry. When the oranges reached the ground, the poor hawker was bewildered. This was the way some of us got it back on the hawkers as they had previously sold us bottles of whiskey which contained weak tea. ✹

Landing British troops from the transports at the Dardanelles under the protection of the battleships (courtesy Trenching at Gallipoli)

 chapter twelve

The Newfoundland Regiment was among the last to leave the Gallipoli Peninsula on January 9, 1916. The Battle Honour "Gallipoli 1915-16" was subsequently approved for emblazonment on the Regimental Colours.

Following the evacuation from Helles, the Regiment was sent to Egypt and defense duty in the Suez Canal, preparatory to proceeding to France and the western battle front.

The Gallipoli and Dardanelles Campaign was a combined British and French naval and military undertaking intended to force a passage through the Dardanelles in order to gain contact with Russian allies and to capture Constantinople from Turkey.

With armies on the Western Front bogged down in trench warfare, Winston Churchill, Britain's First Lord of the Admiralty, proposed an attack to capture Constantinople and knock Turkey out of the war.

The immediate objectives were to supply Russia with munitions, war material and other assistance, open a line of communication for grain and food supplies from the Black Sea to the Mediterranean, win Bulgaria to the side of the Allies, and strengthen the prestige of the Allies in the Middle East.

The campaign was begun in February, 1915, exclusively as a naval venture.

A British-French fleet was concentrated off Limnos Island in the northern Aegean Sea, about 60 miles from the entrance to the Dardanelles Strait, which was heavily mined and guarded on both sides by Turkish forts.

By March, the Allied fleet was forced to admit defeat.

The Allied High Command then decided that land forces would have to assume the dominant role in the campaign if the Allies were to gain possession of the strait.

The Allied forces began their landings on the morning of April 25, under exceedingly difficult conditions, as six Turkish divisions commanded by German general Otto Liman von Sanders were positioned effectively on the Gallipoli Peninsula.

Allied forces numbering 75,000 men landed at dawn April 25th.

The British 29th Division, to which the Newfoundland Regiment was later attached, fought its way ashore at Cape Helles, at the tip of the Gallipoli Peninsula. .

Australia and New Zealand Army Corps — the initials spelled Anzac — gained a foothold on what came to be known as Anzac Cove, 14 miles up the coast, near Suvla Bay.

At the same time, the British Navy and a French division carried out diversionary tactics.

The end result of all that concerted effort was that the Allies made no headway against the entrenched enemy forces and a period of trench warfare began.

There was an Allied plan to send further reinforcements to Gallipoli, but the plan was dropped when the turn of events in the Balkans became critical for the Allied forces.

Between September and December, the French and British governments considered the withdrawal of troops from Gallipoli.

On Dec. 8, 1915, orders were dispatched to Sir Charles Carmichael Munro, who had succeeded Sir Ian Hamilton, to withdraw from Suvla Bay. A week later an order came to evacuate Cape Helles. The evacuation was completed on January 9.

The struggle for the Dardanelles ended in complete failure for the Allies. Some of the evacuated troops were sent to Salonika, but most were dispatched to Egypt for reassignment to other fronts.

In Gallipoli, the Allies and Turkey each lost about 100,000 men killed, wounded or missing.

What Beaumont Hamel is to Newfoundland, so Gallipoli is to Australia and New Zealand.

It was in Gallipoli that members of the Australian and New Zealand Army died in the thousands in one of the most futile campaigns of the First World War.

When the Newfoundland Regiment was withdrawn from the Helles beaches during the final evacuation of Gallipoli, more than two weeks passed before they reassembled in Suez. Massive movement of evacuating Allied troops and equipment led to delays which prevented the entire Regiment from reaching Suez until July 17.

When the Regiment finally mustered before Lieutenant- Colonel A. Hadow, their newly appointed commanding officer, they were a force of only 487 men.

The Newfoundland Regiment had suffered almost 700 casualties in Gallipoli, of whom more than 300 were recuperating in hospitals located in England and various points in the Mediterranean, including Alexandria and Cairo.

Visiting the wounded was one of the tasks undertaken by the Newfoundland War Contingent Association. Formed in September 1915 by friends of Newfoundland living in Great Britain, the Association's first chairman was Sir Edgar Bowring, and its primary goal was to look after the well being of the men of the Newfoundland Regiment.

In addition to finding out about wounded Newfoundlanders arriving in Great Britain and keeping in touch with them, the Association arranged with the Red Cross to have the Newfoundlanders in the Mediterranean visited in hospital.

As well as visiting and keeping in touch with the wounded, the Association was concerned with distributing socks and other items of clothing sent over from Newfoundland by the Women's Patriotic Association.

By the middle of 1918, nearly 30,000 pairs of socks, 1,500 shirts, 6,500 pairs of mittens, 4,000 scarves and more than one million cigarettes had been distributed to the boys overseas. ✺

Cleaning up after coming down from the trenches at Suvla (courtesy Trenching at Gallipoli)

 chapter thirteen

Those members of the Newfoundland Regiment sent to Suez spent two months in defense duty, and gained a reputation for loading mules faster than any other battalion in the 29th Division.

The honour of being the fastest mule loaders went to the burly Goodyear brothers from Grand Falls. At the loading platform, Transport Sergeant Stan Goodyear and his brother, Joe, would stand on either side of the ramp, stripped to the waist. Their method of loading mules was to link their arms behind the animal's rump and run it up the ramp and on to the flat car.

The Transport Section established a new record and boasted proudly "We'll show them how to load mules."

Jim Stacey was among those who spent time in Suez.

Egypt
It was not too long a trip by train to Suez. The Twenty-ninth Division was the first white troop to billet there. We had to put up our own tents on the desert. Many of the Indian Troops, the camel corps, were building roads, as

Suez was to become the Head Quarters for the Palestine campaign later in the war. It was interesting for us to see the Indians building roads and how they lived and worked. Most of the labour battalions were also made up of Indians.

We were at Suez quite a long time before we were paid and we had to be content with our rations of bully beef and biscuits. We were finally paid January 18 in Egyptian money. As there was a canteen close by, operated by the natives, one could get iced lemonade for a penny a glass, camel's butter that did not look too appetizing as it was opened to the dust and flies, oranges, tomatoes and cigarettes. There was a Regiment of Gurkhas, the only Indian soldiers like ourselves who I noticed, liked their fags. They were paying one half peseta for a package of ten, the same kind that I had brought off the Peninsula. So I approached them, as they were about to buy some from the canteen. Now I had funds to buy tomatoes and oranges of which I was very fond. We would also go to the bazaar, where most everything in eastern style was on display. To relate a story: As we used Egyptian money, one hundred pesetas to the pound, a peseta was worth about five cents in our money and when you changed the equivalent of one pound, you had a double handful of a mixture of white silver or nickel coins. They were all marked in Arabic and we could not tell the value.

A five peseta was silver and a half peseta was nickel. They were both the same size and only the five pesetas had a milled edge. Money was a problem with some of the boys. The natives would do you in if you did not watch them closely. Once I was buying some tomatoes and asked for two pounds. The customer before me had bought one pound and I noticed the weights on the scale were not changed for my two pounds.

After payday we would go to Suez which was about two miles away from camp. The Egyptian oversized boys would have the only transport to camp, "donkeys". Going home, some would hire them for pleasure and others because they could not walk. You would get on the donkey and the boy would run along with a stick to keep the donkey moving. Some of the Egyptian boys who had not fared too well (and I suppose were broke) would say in broken English, "Gibet money for donk". It would not be strange to see half a dozen donkeys tied up to the guard tent the next morning after payday. I never rode one, always used shank's mare. After all it was a relief from the trenches.

Hadow, who was the 88th Brigade Major, took over in the trenches as Lt. Col. De H. Burton, our Commanding Officer was too old. We were in for a good hard training session which was absolutely necessary to make us fit. Route marches over the desert under the hot sun were often on the battalion orders and were not liked by many of us. Some showed their resentment to Hadow, which he knew about and confirmed when I visited him in 1961.

I will relate a story I heard while stationed at Suez. Three soldiers who were broke and hungry went into a restaurant, ordered three meals and ate them. When the one who placed the order was presented with the bill, he began to argue as to who was to pay for them and all three started taking off their tunics as if to fight. The poor proprietor was bewildered and as he did not want his place broken up he ushered them all out through the door, so their plan paid off.

We often took walks to Port Tewfick, a port on the Red Sea; a Company at a time, to get deloused and have a shower bath. While having the shower, our clothing was taken and put into a steam boiler and steamed for half an hour so that everything that crawled or otherwise was put to death with the heat. I wondered sometimes if the heat hatched the nits, as there were just as many around afterwards. We had to do guard duty at areas such as the fresh water canal. I was chosen for this duty. When the sun goes down in this part of the world, it gets cold in a hurry. On this particular occasion we were good and cold. We had a brazier but no wood, so we scouted around to see what we could find. We found some wooden supports used to keep up vines. We took some and built a fire and had it cozy for the rest of the night. Before we left the next morning, the owner of the vines accused us of taking the supports, but the Sergeant told him that he was wrong. The owner then pointed to the trail that we had made in hauling them over to the camp. What could we say? ⚙

Washing Day in Wartime Gallipoli (courtesy Trenching at Gallipoli)

Landing Party at the Dardanelles (courtesy Trenching at Gallipoli)

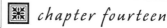 *chapter fourteen*

The military operations of World War I began on three major European fronts: the Western or Franco-Belgian; the Eastern or Russian; and the Southern or Serbian.

When Turkey entered the war on the side of the Central Powers, fighting took place between Turkey and Russia in the Caucasus, and between Turkey and Great Britain at the Dardanelles and in Turkish-held Mesopotamia.

Before the end of 1914, two more fronts had been established: the Austro-Italian, after Italy entered the war on the side of the Allies; and, after Bulgaria entered the war on the enemy side, a front on the Greek frontier, north of Salonika.

The German plan at the start of the war was to defeat France quickly in the West while a small part of the German army and the entire Austro-Hungarian army held the Russians in check in the East.

The speedy defeat of France was to be accomplished by the "Schlieffen Plan" a strategic objective drawn up by Count Alfred von Schlieffen, German chief of staff from 1891 to 1907. The Schlieffen Plan called for

German forces to sweep through Belgium, out-flank the French by their rapid movement, then wheel about, surround and destroy them.

The swift German move into Belgium at the beginning of August routed the Belgian army, which abandoned the strongholds of Liege and Namur, and took safety in the fortress at Antwerp.

The Germans then rushed onwards, defeating the French at Charleroi and the British Expeditionary Force of 90,000 men at Mons, and causing the entire allied line in Belgium to retreat.

At the same time the Germans drove the French out of Lorraine and back from the borders of Luxembourg. the British and French quickly fell back to the Marne River.

Three German armies advanced to the Marne and crossed the river.

The fall of Paris seemed so imminent that the French government moved to Bordeaux.

However, after the Germans crossed the Marne, the French, under General Joseph Joffre, wheeled around Paris and attacked.

In the first Battle of the Marne, September 6-9, the French succeeded in halting the Germans, which resulted in a general German retreat to the Aisne River. The French then engaged the Germans in three battles: the Battle of the Aisne, a battle on the Somme River, and the first Battle of Arras.

But the Germans could not be dislodged, and even extended their line eastwards to the Meuse, north of Verdun.

A race to the North Sea then took place, with the objective being the Channel ports.

The Belgians prevented the Germans from advancing to the French Channel ports by flooding the region around the Yser River.

The western part of the Allied line was held by the British who, in the race for the Channel, had advanced to Ypres, the southwest corner of Belgium.

After taking Antwerp on October 10, the Germans tried to break through the British positions in Belgium, but were checked in a series of engagements known collectively as the Battle of Flanders.

In December, the Allies attacked along the entire front, but failed to make any real gains.

By the end of 1914, both sides had established lines extending about 500 miles from Switzerland to the North Sea and had entrenched. These lines were to remain almost stationary for the next three years.

The Battle of Flanders marked the end of fighting in the open in the West.

From the end of 1914, until almost the close of the war in 1918, fighting consisted largely of trench warfare, with each side laying seige to the other's system of trenches (consisting of numerous parallel lines of inter-communicating trenches protected by lines of barbed wire), and attempting to break through the lines.

The principal attempts to force a breakthrough in 1915 included a British attack at Neuve Chapelle in March, which took only the German advance line.

In April, the Germans unsuccessfully attacked Ypres, using clouds of chlorine gas, the first time in history gas was used in this manner on a large scale.

In May and June, a combined attack by the British and French along the front between Neuvre Chapelle and Arraas advanced the Allies 2.5 miles into the German trench system, but did not secure a breakthrough.

Unsuccessful attacks by the British and French in September were unable to take the town of Lens and Vimy Ridge.

In September, a French attack on a front of 15 miles between Reims and the Argonne Forest, took the Germans first line of trenches, but was stopped at the second.

For the most part, the lines that had been established in the West at the close of 1914 remained much the same during 1915.

In 1916, the success of the Germans in thrusting the Russians back from East Prussia, Galicia and Poland, enabled the Germans to transfer roughly 500,000 men from the Eastern to the Western Front for an attempt to force a decision.

The German plan was to attack the French fortress at Verdun in great strength, in an attempt to weaken the French. The Allied plan for 1916, as laid out by General Joffre of France and General Haig of Great Britain, was to break through the German lines in the West by means of a powerful British/French offensive.

The Allied offensive was to take place during the summer in the region of the Somme River.

By March of 1916, the general opinion was that the Newfoundland Regiment's next move would be to France.

Great things were being planned for the Western Front that summer.

The year 1915 had ended badly for the Allies.

Their offensive in Artois and Champagne hadn't worked. On the Eastern Front, an Austrian- German drive had pushed the Russians back almost 100 miles to Warsaw. The Gallipoli campaign had failed. The Suez Canal still faced a Turkish threat, and in Mesopotamia, a combined British and Indian force was under siege in Kur-el-Amara, which was to fall before the end of April. This sequence of reversals made the Allies realize the need for a united aim.

At an Allied military conference held in Chantilly, France, in December, 1915, it was unanimously agreed that the war could only be decided by big offensives launched in the principal theatres in the greatest possible strength.

What this meant was that France would be the main fighting front for troops of the British Empire. [18]

All efforts were then concentrated on building up the forces of Sir Douglas Haig, the British Commander in Chief on the Western Front. As a result, the 29th British Division, which the Newfoundland Regiment was attached to, was one of many brought home from Egypt.

At the December conference in Chantilly, France's General Joffre had proposed to Haig that the principal French-British offensive for 1916 should be a 60-mile front astride the River Somme.

In the interest of Allied unity, Haig went along with Joffre even though his preference was for an attack in Flanders assisted by a landing on the Belgian coast in the rear of the Germans.

The joint British/French offensive was set to be launched on July 1, 1916.

The Allied plan for 1916 was to launch simultaneous offenses on the Western, Eastern and Italian Fronts. In the West, the region of the Somme was chosen as the site for a joint French and British assault, but the Allied plan was upset in February when German General Erich von Falkenhayn unleashed one of the most powerful offensives of the war against the French city of Verdun.

The Battle of Verdun lasted for five months and, at the end of it, a total of 800,000 Allied and German troops had died.

French soldiers referred to the Battle of Verdun as "the mincing machine." It minced the very heart out of the French army and reduced its contributions to the Somme offensive from 40 divisions to 16, of which only five attacked on July 1.

During the Battle of Verdun, the French appealed to Haig to hasten the Somme offensive.

With French forces virtually decimated at Verdun, the weight of the Somme offensive would now fall to the British, with General Joffre's originally planned front of 60 miles shortened to 24.

The planned area of Allied attack reached from the German held village of Gommecourt to a point four miles south of the River Somme.

On March 15, the Newfoundland Regiment, including Jim Stacey, departed Suez enroute to France and the Western Front.

On March 16th, we said good bye to all our pleasures and sorrows and boarded the S.S. Alaunia (Cunard Liner of 13,000 tons) at Port Tewfick. We were on our way through the Canal to Marseilles, our destination, on the south coast of France. We had an uneventful trip through the Mediterranean Sea. It was my first and last time to be "on crime" since on active service. The crime was being asleep when there was deck drill. For this I received five days of extra fatigue.

After a voyage of six days, the Alaunia steamed into the French harbour of Marseilles.

Disembarkation began after breakfast and by noon all the men and equipment were ashore.

At 6 p.m. the troops boarded trains which brought them ultimately to their destination of Pont Remy, where they left the train and fell in to march to their billets.

Along the way they had to march over bridge which crossed the River Somme.

At the time they had no way of knowing this was their introduction to war at its worst.

On April 1, a ten-mile march brought the Newfoundland Regiment to Bonneville, a village 15 miles north of Amiens. From Bonneville, they marched to Louvencourt.

The change in billets marked the 29th Division's taking over a sector of the British front line.

The 29th Division was now in the British Fourth Army, commanded by General Sir Henry Rawlinson, and forming part of the Eighth Corps, under the command of Lieutenant-General Sir Aylmer Hunter-Weston, who had been the officer in charge of the 29th in Gallopoli.

By the time the 29th Division arrived from the Mediterranean, the initial plans for the Somme offensive had changed from a 60-mile line of attack to a 24-mile front line, extending from Gommecourt to a point four miles north of the Somme. British forces held 18 miles of this front; their boundary with the French ran through the village of Maricourt, two miles north of the Somme.

The Fourth Army was responsible for a 14-mile front, stretching from Maricourt to a mile beyond Serre. The northern boundary of this sector ran from within a mile of Beaumont Hamel, on the right bank of the Ancre River, to the army boundary. The Germans held the whole of this front in considerable strength. The first line of enemy defense consisted of three rows of trenches. There was as well a second line of defense and a third was being worked on.

The Germans had built redoubts, thick concrete forts well fortified with guns, to guard worrisome spots. There were redoubts on Redan Ridge and Hawthorn Ridge. The Heidenkopf, a square of reinforced and covered trenches, guarded the road between the villages of Beaumont Hamel and Serre.

South of the little village of Beaumont Hamel, just behind the German front line of trenches, there was a natural feature, a deep chasm. which is known in military history as the "Y Ravine." This huge chasm provided the Germans with a well hidden sanctuary in which they'd situated large dugouts and machine guns.

Major-General Sir Beauvoir de Lisle, commander of the 29th

Division, established divisional headquarters at Acheux, putting his reserve brigade in billets in nearby Louvencourt. Other reserve forces were quartered in the small villages of Englebelmer and Mailly Maillet, two miles behind the front lines.

When de Lisle took over his sector early in April, he placed the 88th Brigade in divisional reserve, so it was to Louvencourt that the men of the Newfoundland Regiment came on April 4.

At this time there was increased emphasis on anti-gas training, which included wearing gas helmets in a chlorine filled chamber for a period of 10 minutes.

Jim Stacey's memories of France begin with his arrival in Marseilles.

France and the Somme

On March 22nd we reached Marseilles and boarded a train at 9:30 PM. This was a nice sunny place and I remember the peach trees in bloom. We were on the train for two days, as we did not move very fast. When we stopped, there would be a big boiler of coffee ready (French style) with brandy mixed in it. I thought it was good; many thought it was good coffee spoiled. Arriving at Pont Remy, close to Abbeville, we detrained. It was much colder here than in the south of France.

We were soon on the march. Our first stop was Buigny L'Abbe, a small village where we rested. While here, on March 29th, we were paid twenty-five francs. That was the last time a Private received twenty-five francs, as there were too many unfit to march the next morning; after that fifteen francs was the pay. We were marching for nearly a week, stopping at villages for the night. Finally we arrived at Louvencourt which was to be our home while in reserves. For the next three months we would stay a week in reserves, then move about two miles up toward the line for a week in supports at Englebelmer and from there to the front line.

The town of Louvencourt was in a quiet section of the countryside, where the ground was tilled and the wheat was planted. It was not too far from the front line, and located in the Valley of the Somme. We were soon to discover that it would lose its quietness. Shortly after our arrival there, I was told to report to Battalion Headquarters. That is when I discovered that I was to be a Battalion runner with three others, one from each Company: Harry Rowe, "B" Company; Walter Thistle, "A" Company; and Jacobs, "C" Company. Our job was to deliver messages to Company Commanders, Medical Officers, Transport section and Brigade Headquarters. I was attached to Battalion Headquarters and only returned to my Company for pay. I retained all of my pay books as they were filled and I still have them. You can see the OC and Paymaster signatures, such as that of the first one, Capt. W. March. A number of the signatures represent those who did not get clear of the battlefield, while many of the others have gone since.

Beaumont Hamel

I spoke to a First World War veteran in the regular British Army who said that he would not have been Battalion runner by choice because it was a dangerous job. We had to be guides for reinforcements, when they arrived at the railhead from the Base. We also had to deliver messages, wherever required, at any time of the day or night, often with little knowledge of where we would find the persons to whom they were addressed. For my part, the advances the Battalion made did not always develop into a general advance, and resulted in situations similar to the Beaumont Hamel stand of July 1st 1916. Sometimes you would get lost but made it a point not to give up; often you would get into embarrassing situations, when moving into new billets behind the line. The Officers would have their sleeping quarters in different occupied houses. In the night you would receive a message for all Battalion Companies. Madame of the house and Officers would have gone to bed. You would open the front door and walk in knowing a certain Officer was in one of the upstairs rooms. You would not know which one, so you would open one door in the dark and be confronted by Madame in her nightdress. She would point to the room saying, "Officer ici".

The other three runners are gone, I am the only one left. Of the Orderly staff, Mac (Malcolm) Godden was in charge with W.J Eaton as clerk. Capt. A. Raley was the Adjunct (I had a letter from him recently, dated October 31, 1962. He is not doing very well. He has heart trouble). Eaton and Mac Godden have passed on to the other side, "C. Fip" (Charles Parsons) of signals is still with us and Art Hammond, the Red Cross Sergeant, is still in the land of the living. Lt. Col. A.H. Hadow was our Commanding Officer with Major Forbes-Robertson his second in command. Brigadier General Cayley was in charge of the 88th Brigade which was comprised of four Battalions: 1st Essex, 2nd Hants, 4th Worcesters and the Newfoundland Regiment. The 88th Brigade together with the 86th and 87th Brigades made up the Twenty-ninth Division under General de Lisle.

From the end of March to July 1st, 1916, we (88 Brigade) held the line in front of Beaumont Hamel. Occasionally the Germans would give our line a strafing for about half an hour at a time and then things would drift back into the same old pattern. When we were out in reserves, the working parties were always on the go, putting up barbed wire and digging saps and dugouts under ground. As a matter of fact, our position was just as strong as that of the enemy and if they had attacked us, they would have met the same fate as we did on July 1st. We had our pleasures when back behind the lines. We held inter Battalion football matches and on those occasions Mick Smythe would mount a mule, belonging to the Transport, bedecked with ribbons and he would lead the Regiment to the grounds where the match was played. There were others who sought out leisure in a different way. Some entered a cafe one night and stole a barrel of beer. To hide it, they sank it in a pond close by and at night would raise it and toast the Regiment, then roll it back again. The *authorities never did find the offenders, but when payday came around so much was taken from each one to pay for it. Reinforcements started to come in to the railhead at Acheux. Often I was there as a guide to bring them to the Battalion. The pattern continued: reserves supports and front line. We would leave Englebelmer for the front line passing through Tipperary Avenue, which traversed a common field, and bearing to the left, the village of Auchonvillers. Bearing left again, we would pass through an orchard to a sunken road, then under the high ground just before Haymarket, the beginning of our trench system.*

Battalion Headquarters was located in this area and it was here that the rats were so tame, they would help themselves to our rations. We disapproved of this and tried every means to get rid of them. Sometimes the boot would be on the other foot, when we would expose ourselves on top of the trench, then Fritz would give us a burst of machine gun fire.

There were four cookers manned by Regimental cooks (one for each Company) and they did a very good job considering the circumstances. The same water that cooked our "skilly" was used to boil our tea. You could be sure that the tea went down easily, because it was well greased.

This is where Easu Penny wrote his famed ditties, "Ideal Milk" and "Number Nine".

When I am dead and quite forgotten,
On my tombstone carve this line:
"Esau Penny, first Newfoundlander,
Mortally wounded by a number nine."

Once while I was in supports at Englebelmer I was given a message to deliver to the Brigade, but was not quite sure where I would find them (as it often happened when moving into a new sector). I started off on the bicycle and was halted by a sentry, who took me before the Commanding Officer. I was asked some searching questions such as, to what Division, Brigade and Battalion did I belong. There were a host of other similar questions. The upshot was, they thought I was a spy.

I would look toward, across, and past the German line and I would scan the landscape, beyond the rising ground, from sunken Beaumont Hamel. There were the same landmarks; a small copse with a house alongside, a lone tree and everything seemed so quiet, that your thoughts would be taken away from the war. The landscape was the same every day. You would think, "surely this is not war."

When June came, everything began to change. Our planes became more numerous. I once counted as many as thirty in the air at one time and they would continually strafe enemy positions. Raids also would be carried out at night on the German front line. There were trench maps showing every detail. Seeing so much activity from our side and so little from the enemy, one would think it would be a walkover. We blasted the Germans for a whole week before July 1st with a steady barrage of shellfire. We moved up the day before from Louvencourt, bidding goodbye to Grandmere, Madame and the Garcon where we had been staying when out of the line. You could see tears in their eyes.

When we first arrived at Louvencourt, there was a notice on Battalion's orders for the day, for all "hard rock" miners to report to Headquarters. I never gave it a thought at the time, as once before they asked for sheet metal workers. On that occasion, it was near Christmas, they were needed to cut down the large tin biscuit containers to make pans to roast the Turkeys. They, the 'hard rock' miners, were needed to dig a sap from our front line out under no-mans-land toward the German front line. This work was carried on until the 1st of July when the mine was exploded. An explosion occurred that would be the signal for the action to start. We were so efficient that, the night before, we had wooden bridges laid across our front line where the wire was cut. This action helped the German machine gunners. All they had to do was to set their sights on the gaps in the wire as we advanced from St. John's Road.

We took up our position in the St. John's Road trench behind the line. Battalion Headquarters was in the centre with "A" and "C" Companies on the left and "B" and "D" Companies on the right. ❀

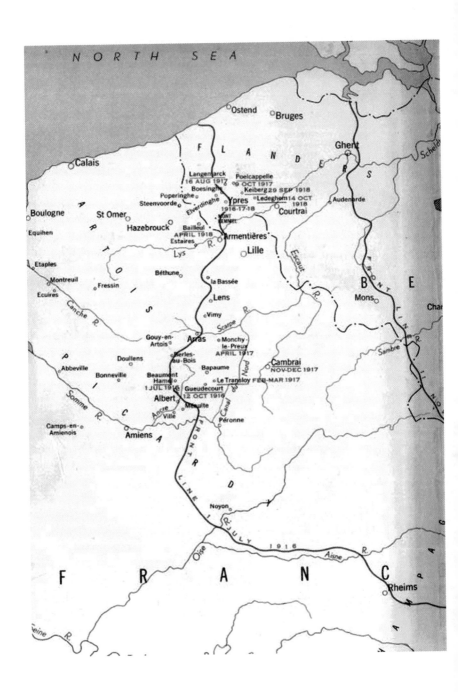

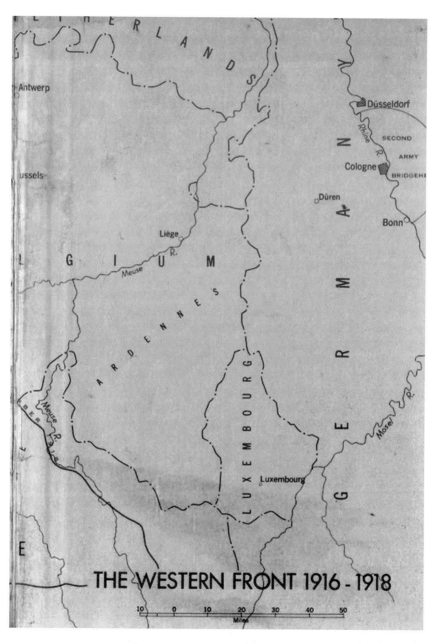

THE WESTERN FRONT 1916 - 1918

(courtesy The Fighting Newfoundlander)

The Three Runners: Walter Thistle,
Will Eaton and Jim Stacey.

✳ *chapter fifteen*

On April 22, 1916, Easter Saturday, the Newfoundland Regiment's Companies C and D, backed up by Companies A and B, entered the firing line for the first time since Gallipoli, taking over 400 yards of trenches from the Worcestershire Regiment.

From their location the men could peer through trench periscopes across a grassy field which sloped down gradually to the barbed wire fences that guarded the German positions, just 300 to 500 yards away.

On April 24, Lieutenant Peter Cashin was wounded by a bullet from a German sniper.

That same day Private George Curnew became the Regiment's first fatality in France when he was struck and killed by an enemy bullet.

In late May, Frank Lind's letter to the Daily News was about the enemy:

The Germans sometimes try to be funny, he told his readers in Newfoundland. When the Australians arrived in the trenches a sign went up from the enemy trenches "Welcome Australians and sons of convicts." When the Newfoundlanders arrived, the sign said "Hello, red man."

In his chatty way, Lind wrote about the men he served with. He mentioned "popular Stan Goodyear, our best boxer and wrestler, strong as an ox" and Stan's brother, "Joe Goodyear, another trump."

He spoke of Captain George Carty, who "the boys fairly worship."

He mentioned Howard Clark who got a shrapnel wound in the head but whose steel helmet saved his life, and "good hearted, genial Peter Cashin."

Lind went on to speculate about how difficult it was going to be to get used to civilian life after the war was over and the boys were back home.

During June, the Newfoundland Regiment was put through hours of rigorous training as they prepared for battle. Men worked as well on improving the trenches and completing underground dugouts that were to accommodate as many as 1,000 men on the night before the upcoming attack. At night, across No Man's Land, the Germans could be heard working on their defenses.

During the last week of June, the 29th Division carried out eight night raids into No Man's Land in an effort to test enemy defenses and capture prisoners.

On two nights, June 26 and 27, a party of 57 Newfoundlanders under Captain Bert Butler, the Newfoundland Regiment's intelligence officer, took part in the night raids. On the second night they made it as far as the enemy's trench but were forced to retreat without a prisoner. Casualties of the operation included four Newfoundlanders killed, 21 wounded, and three missing.

Captain Butler and Private George Phillips of Whitbourne, who was credited with bayoneting two Germans, were both awarded the Military Medal for their part in the raids.

In a letter to the Daily News, Frank Lind wrote with pride of the Regiment's honour and said Captain Butler was the bravest man he'd ever seen.

On June 26, General de Lisle addressed the Newfoundland Regiment.

He spoke of the strength of the Fourth Army's artillery, the 45,000 tons of ammunition shells ready for the upcoming battle, and said the Fourth Army's 263 battalions would be facing only 32 German battalions.

Listening to the general, the men felt confident of a swift victory.

On June 29, Frank Lind ended his letter to the Daily News: *Tell everyone that they may feel proud of the Newfoundland Regiment for we get nothing but praise from the Divisional General down. Kind regards.*

On June 30, the eve of the Battle of Beaumont Hamel, Lieutenant Owen Steele of St. John's, wrote in his daily journal: *I believe the climax of our troubles will be reached within the next few days, after which the day of peace will quickly draw near though they will undoubtedly bring trouble to many.*

He signed off, This will be my last letter for a short while. [23]

June 30 of 1916 was a beautiful day.

At 9 p.m. a total of 801 Newfoundlanders, including 66 untried reinforcements who had arrived from the Ayr depot in Scotland that day, together with their commanding officer, Colonel Hadow, marched out of Louvencourt.

For the first 200 yards, the men marched at attention.

When Hadow gave the signal to march at ease, the troops broke into the song, "Keep the Home Fire Burning."

East of Acheux, the Regiment halted for half an hour waiting for total darkness, then crossed the open fields south of Mailly-Maillet, accompanied by the sound of British guns pounding the German positions. The men finally arrived at the entrance to Tipperary Avenue, the deep communication trench they had helped build.

It was after 2 a.m. when the Newfoundland Regiment settled down in their 750-yard section of the St. John's Road trench, directly opposite the "Y Ravine."

The plan for the following day's battle was that the 29th Division's 86th and 87th Brigades would clear the way: the 86th on the left, in front of Beaumont Hamel; the 87th on the right, in front of the Y Ravine.

Their objective was to capture the German's front line trench position, extending from Beaumont Hamel along Station Road.

They would then proceed to their second objective, the German intermediate line on the Beaucourt to Beaumont Hamel road.

With this accomplished, the 29th's 88th Brigade, which included the Newfoundland Regiment, would pass through the other two brigades and advance beyond them to finish the job.

According to the proposed battle plan, the final half mile surge towards Puisieux Trench would begin at three hours and ten minutes after zero hour.

During the night of June 30, the 29th Division was busy assembling in its battle stations.

Each man was equipped with a minimum load of 66 pounds, which included a haversack containing shaving gear, extra socks, and food; special emergency rations; a gas helmet and goggles; field dressings and iodine; a rolled ground sheet; a water bottle; a steel helmet; wire cutters; a mess tin; two sandbags, and a rifle.

Most also carried extra items including shovels, picks, wire, extra bombs and flares. [24]

In the early hours of July 1, a hot breakfast was brought up from the regimental cookers assembled in woods near Englebelmer.

From then on, it was just a matter of waiting in the cold and damp.

Officers walked around making final inspections. Men dozed, smoked and chatted.

At 6:25 a.m. an intense bombardment began.

An officer from each battalion went to the Brigade Major to synchronize watches.

Zero hour was 65 minutes away.

In planning the day's battle, special attention had been made to deal with the Hawthorn Redoubt, a strong point in the German front line on the crest of Hawthorn Ridge directly opposite Beaumont Hamel.

During weeks of excavation, Allied troops had tunneled deep under No Man's Land to set a charge of 40,000 pounds of ammunition 65 feet beneath the Hawthorn Redoubt.

The exact time of the explosion had been a matter of great discussion.

General Hunter-Weston had proposed it be blown four hours before the attack began, at 3:30 a.m. He reasoned this would allow the resulting crater to be occupied before the main attack began. The four hour interval between the explosion and attack might also lull the enemy into a sense of false security.

A compromise order finally set the actual time of detonation at ten minutes before zero hour.

Promptly at 7:20 a.m. the mine went off and from 1,000 yards away the Newfoundlanders watched as a huge spewing of earth, stones and debris shot into the air.

When the mine went off on Hawthorn Ridge, the Germans realized only too clearly that an infantry attack was imminent and they prepared for battle.

What the Germans saw they as they peered over No Man's Land is recorded in their regimental history.

"The explosion was a signal for the infantry attack, and everyone got ready and stood on the lower steps of the dugouts, rifles in hand, waiting for the bombardment to life. In a few minutes the shelling ceased, and we rushed up the steps and out into the crater positions. Ahead of us wave after wave of British troops were crawling out of their trenches and coming towards us at a walk, their bayonets glistening in the sun." [25]

From left to right of the 29th Division's front, the soldiers the Germans saw advancing towards them were the 1st Battalion Lancashire Fusiliers, the 2nd Battalion Royal Fusiliers, the 2nd Battalion South Wales Borderers and the 1st Battalion King's Own Rifles.

Within five minutes, the assault companies were practically annihilated.

At 8:45 a.m. Brigadier-General Cayley issued orders by telephone to the Newfoundland and Essex Regiments to advance as soon as possible.

The question as to whether the enemy's first line trench had been taken was answered with the reply that the situation was not cleared up.

It was apparent the 29th Division's attack was not going according to plan. Nevertheless, at 9:15 a.m. the Newfoundlanders advanced from St. John's Road trench. The men were alone in their advance. Trenches clogged with the dead and dying delayed the Essex Regiment's attack until almost 10 a.m.

From a starting position in St. John's Road, the Newfoundland Regiment had to cross 250 yards of fire-swept ground before they reached their own front line. Then there were four belts of their own barbed wire to get through. The wire had been pre-cut with zig zag gaps made few and narrow as a means of concealing the men from the enemy. Now, in the midst of battle, it was found there were too few gaps to pass through. Not only was the Regiment's advance impeded, but the gaps were quickly discovered by the Germans who trained their guns on them with terrible results.

In the regimental diary, Colonel Hadow wrote that while the enemy's fire was effective from the outset, from the moment the men went over the top, the heaviest casualties occurred as they were passing through the gaps in their own front wire. It was there, he wrote, that "men were mown down in heaps."

Members of the Regiment who succeeded in making it through the barbed wire could look down an incline and see the for the first time the barrier of the German wire guarding the enemy trenches. Half way down the slope, in an area where the enemy's shrapnel was particularly deadly, was what came to be known as the Danger Tree.

Before the deadly day ended, the muddy, churned up ground near the trunk of the Danger Tree would be filled with the bodies of dead and dying Newfoundlanders.

It was here that Frank "Mayo" Lind was killed.

Some of the many, many others who died on that terrible day included Edward Carrigan of Placentia, Edward Butler of Fogo, George Hawkins of Twillingate, Silas Jeffers of Bay de Verde, Roberts Simms from St. Anthony, Josiah Smith of Hopeall, Harvey Harris of Burgeo, Gilbert Antle of Botwood, Harold Hutchens of Greenspond, Michael Jackman of Grand Falls, Lawrence Murphy from Petty Harbour, George Newhook of Dildo, Horatio Barbour of Port Rexton, Maxwell Janes of St. John's, and Richard Pittman from Lamaline.

The attack started an hour before we went over. While waiting in the trench, spent machine gun bullets fell at our feet. An officer of the 87th

Brigade jumped down in the trench and went to Battalion Headquarters. Seeing the look on his face, a feeling of misgiving went through me. Just after that, the Adjutant came out with two messages. One was given to me for the Company Commanders of "B" and "D" Companies and another orderly received a message for "A" and "C" Companies. I delivered the message to Captain Bruce Reid of "B" Company and Captain Eric Ayre of "D" Company. That was the last message they received, because a few minutes later they stepped upon the parapet and advanced in two waves, when Hadow came out and waved his hand, at about 9:00 a.m. St. John's Road trench was about two hundred yards behind the front line. They could not see the start of the advance from there. As I stated earlier, the wire had been cut in our front line and bridges laid across the trench the night before. This was a death trap for our boys as the enemy just set the sights of their machine guns on the gaps in the barbed wire and fired. A short while later, Battalion Headquarters staff followed the Advance. Hadow, Raley, the Signalmen, the Red Cross and the Runners carried on just past our own barbed wire and lay down to see the results. I could see no one moving, but heaps of Khaki slumped on the ground. Raley saw a man crawling into our trench on the left and he said to me, "Stacey, go along the trench and see what you can find out from him". I started to push my way through the trench (one had to keep to the trench because of machine gun fire) but, it was filled with the wounded, and as I tried to push by the wounded, agonizing cries would come from them. It was too much for me so I turned and went back and told Raley it was impossible. We stayed there for a while because it was useless to go forward, as it seemed that everyone was wiped out.

Hadow told us to go back, which we did. He was also able to stop the 4th Worcesters Regiment from going over. By this time Fritz was sending the big one, HE (high explosives) over. Shrapnel would burst just over our heads (which accounted for so many missing as the HE shells blew the dead and wounded to pieces). We made our way to Hyde Park Corner, which was to the back and right of our sector. When it cooled down later in the day, Jimmy Young and I were sent out to pick up the Regiment stragglers in the trenches and bring them to Hyde Park Corner. It was quite a job and Fritz was still putting over big ones; they did not make you feel good. We picked up a number of men; some were shell-shocked and could not speak. We recognized our own by the letter "N" on their steel helmets. Getting back to Hyde Park Corner with the shell-shocked was no easy task. The trenches were blocked with the wounded and no one wanted to risk climbing on top because the shelling was still heavy, to say no less of machine gun fire. Knowing the trenches part way back and that we could not be seen as the ground sloped from our Front Line, I persuaded all to follow me and made a short cut across the open to Hyde Park Corner. The Quartermaster, Captain Summers, who had come up to get the ration strength for the next day, was taken away wounded; he died the next day. Sgt. Cleary who was with

Summers and who had just come back off leave was killed close to Headquarters. Shortly afterwards (I do not remember too much) I woke up in a dugout. As it was getting dark, I must have crawled there and went to sleep. When I reported to Headquarters, they had me listed as missing.

What was left of the Regiment took up position at St. James Street to the right of our sector. The next day we were going to be relieved. Lt. Col. Hadow called me in, showed me a trench map and explained that the Lincoln Regiment was relieving us that night and I was to be the guide. He showed me the best and shortest way to bring the Regiment up, which was through Picadilly Avenue.

I did not tell him that I was not going to pass through Picadilly Avenue because I had passed that way earlier and an HE (high Explosive) shell had burst in the middle of about twenty of the Worcesters Regiment who were waiting to go over the top. Such a mess cannot be imagined. I happened to pass that way later that day as they were being buried and had to use my pH gas mask.

The following is from a cutting dated July 1963 from a Birmingham England newspaper that was sent to me:

"Although the survivors of the first battle of the Somme Forty Seven years ago today, July 1st, must be a small company, I was one of them. (Mr. A.J. Tye aged seventy-four). Assembling overnight in the assault trench we had a long wait for Zero hour 7:30 a.m. When the Big Mine of Beaumont Hamel was blown up (the Blood Bath on the Somme). This was one of the courageous annals of the British "Tommy". It was also one of the most costly. The British artillery had laid down an intensive barrage for seven days. At seven o'clock in the morning the fierce barrage was increased. Half an hour later came the order to attack. Fifteen British Divisions on the North of the River Somme and five French Divisions on the South went over the top. These were the days of classic warfare. The World's first tank was to be introduced on this front in September 1916 with the infantry advancing in waves with fixed bayonets. The week long barrage that had organized very strong defensive positions forewarned the Germans. That as soon as the barrage lifted to allow the infantry to go in, their Machine gunners in fox holes began taking a heavy toll of the Tommies.

Men were mown down in waves. Whole units were almost wiped out. Shellfire had churned up the whole area and later heavy rain made "Somme mud", the curse of every soldier in the Army. This terrible expensive battle was to go on for four and a half months ending in the capture of Beauport and Beaumont Hamel on November 13th. But that opening day forty seven days ago today brought casualties to the British Army as heavy as on any day during the First World War."

Before the Battalion was relieved the next day, everything was quiet. While *on a message, I took a walk through our front line trench and saw there war at its worst, with the trench full of dead in all kinds of gruesome shapes. Every unit going into battle always left ten percent behind. They would make up an effective Unit after an engagement such as this one.*

When we were relieved, Lt. Owen Steele went down to Englebelmer as billeting officer to have billets all ready when we left the line. The houses close to the line were in bad shape. We had just arrived from the front line, when Lt. Steele and Major Forbes-Robertson who were walking down the centre of the village road, heard a High Explosive shell coming in their direction. Robertson ducked into the ditch on the right hand side of the road and Steele made for the other side, under an old barn. Fate was against Steele as the shell exploded in the barn. He was wounded with a compound fracture of his thigh. The 87th Field Ambulance Unit was stationed at Mailly-Maillet, a village about a mile and a half away, so I jumped on the bicycle to get their help. We left Mailly with the bicycle aboard the ambulance (a Model T Ford). When we had gone a mile, the engine failed so I had to get on the bicycle and go back for another; this time we succeeded and finally managed to get Steele to the Field Ambulance Unit. This was the beginning of the week. In the meantime, we moved to our camp to Mailly Wood. Friday we heard that Steele had died of his wounds. Capt. March asked me to go up to the Shugaree (sous terre) on the main road just outside Mailly, where there was a Military Cemetery with graves already dug and pick out a grave for Steele. I saw the man in charge and selected one. It was arranged for that Sunday that Steele's Company, "D" would attend his funeral. I was the guide and Lt. C. Duley was the officer in charge. I did not know what arrangements had been made to go to the Cemetery. We had to pass the 87th Field Ambulance Unit where he was taken when wounded. As we passed the Ambulance Unit, I mentioned to Duley that perhaps it would be a good idea to go in and check, as there were no signs of any preparations for a funeral. He said, "No", so we carried on, with "D" Company following, to the Shugaree, (Sousperre) to the grave, which I had chosen. There was no one there so we did not fulfill the task we set out to do that is, attend the funeral of Lt. Owen Steele. I did not find out until last year, (1962), where he was buried. I asked his brother in St. John's and he told me he was buried at Mailly, perhaps in the same grave I had chosen.

We moved the orderly room and officers' quarters from Mailly Woods to a chateau which was not occupied by the natives. The grounds of the chateau covered a large area and contained a garden. I noticed there were several beehives. Some were destroyed, but others were in good order. I knew there must be honey in them as they were alive with bees. I wondered how to get the honey out without being stung. Having a pH gas mask I thought, "if it can keep out poison gas, it should keep out bees". It was like a small pillow slip with goggles for the eyes and a nozzle made of rubber pipe that you put in the mouth; the fabric was soaked with chemicals. In the mouth piece there was a valve that closed when you inhaled through your mouth. You had to breathe through your nose, as the air had to come through the fabric and be exhaled through the pipe in your mouth. This is what I put over my head. I put a pair of gauntlets over my hands tied at the wrists. It was not much trouble to get the honey with this rig. I happened to look around and saw some troops walking through the grounds enjoying the pleasant surroundings. The furious bees, which could not show their displeasure at me, must have made an attack on the troops as I saw them running and waving their arms with alarm. I gave the officers a treat of honey and was told that someone owned the bees. (I wonder how they figured that out.)

Back in Englebelmer, just behind the orderly room stood a cherry tree and in July the cherries were ripe. I climbed the tree and had my fill, then filled my steel helmet and gave the staff a treat; fruit was not normally on the menu.

On our last day at Englebelmer a fifteen-inch howitzer was in action on the grounds. It was the first time I had seen such a large gun in action. It was quite a performance watching the crew firing it. "When Grandmere speaks", was the cant they gave it and it sure did speak. When it was fired, you needed cotton wool to put in your ears and you could see, plainly, the shell leave the nozzle.

The July 1 Battle of Beaumont Hamel was a colossal disaster.

At 9:45 that morning, Colonel Hadow reported to Brigade Headquarters that the attack had failed.

By 2 p.m. orders had been given for the attack to be ended and the trenches cleared.

The Newfoundland Regiment suffered 710 casualties at Beaumont Hamel.

The following day, when the roll call of the unwounded was taken, only 68 answered their name.

British troops, overall, suffered a total of 57,470 casualties, more than 19, 000 of which were fatal. For the British, July 1 would turn out to be the bloodiest day of the First World War.

The cost in human life was staggering for an advance into the enemy's position which averaged one mile in depth across a front of some three and a half miles.

What went wrong at Beaumont Hamel was something long debated. Blame was placed on faulty tactical direction from the general staff, and lack of experience among officers, but there was unanimous agreement that no blame for failure could be placed upon the fighting troops.

Whenever the subject of Beaumont Hamel arises, there is always high praise for the courage and discipline of the Newfoundland Regiment in what was their first battle on the Western Front.

In The Fighting Newfoundlander, Colonel Nicholson quotes letters of commendation written to Newfoundland Governor Walter Davidson.

The Commander of the 88th Brigade, Brigadier-General Cayley said:

I was in a position to observe the advance of the Newfoundland Regiment. Nothing could have been finer. In face a devastating shell and machine gun fire, they advanced over our parapets, not a man faltering or hanging back. They literally went on until scarcely an officer or man was left un hit. I cannot sufficiently express my admiration for their heroism nor my sorrow for their overwhelming losses.

Divisional Commander General de Lisle wrote:

It was a magnificent display of trained and disciplined valor, and its assault only failed of success because dead men can advance no farther.

The Commander in Chief, Field Marshal Sir Douglas Haig, sent the following cable:

"Newfoundland may well feel proud of her sons. The heroism and devotion to duty they displayed on 1st July has never been surpassed. Please convey my deep sympathy and that of the whole of our Armies in France in the loss of the brave officers and men who have fallen for the Empire. And our admiration for their heroic conduct. Their efforts contributed to or success, and their example will live." [26]

❋

Four members of the Ayre family who died on July 1, 1916. (Left to right) Captain Eric Ayre, Captain Bernard Ayre, Lieutenant Wilfrid Ayre and Lieutenant Gerald Ayre
(courtesy What Became of Corporal Pittman)

▓ *chapter sixteen*

The people of Newfoundland had no idea of what had happened to the Newfoundland Regiment on July 1.

Five days after the battle, on July 6, The Evening Telegram announced that the British had launched a great offensive on July 1 and that German trenches and prisoners had been captured over a 20-mile front. A report from British headquarters said:

A tremendous British offensive was launched at 7:30 a.m., over a front extending from 20 miles north of the Somme. The British troops already have occupied the German front line and have captured many prisoners. A terrific bombardment which preceded the attack lasted the whole of an hour and a half. It is too early yet to give any particulars of the fighting, which is developing in intensity. The British casualties have so far been comparatively light, according to official reports.

The report concluded:

New British mortars played a great role in cutting wire entanglements and destroying trenches. A large number of prisoners had been taken. Some of the prisoners say the British curtain of fire prevented them from getting food for the past five days.

Another report stated the joint British/French offensive launched on July 1 had resulted in the Allies breaking the German forward defense on a 16-mile front. It was said 7,000 German prisoners had been taken.

Just below, on the same page, there was news that Lord Kitchener, who had been lost at sea when the cruiser, Hampshire, struck a mine and sank, had left an estate valued at £171,420.

A signed letter that Kitchener had written calling for 30,000 recruits had been sold at auction on behalf of the Red Cross to Thomas Fenwick Harris for £6,000.

In the paper's regularly carried casualty list of the Newfoundland Regiment, it was noted that Captain Bertram Butler of Topsail had been slightly wounded but remained on duty and Lieutenant Charles St. Clair of Exploits had been wounded in the cheek.

Private Heber Cuff of Bonavista was reported in "severe condition" in London's Wandsworth Hospital after being wounded in the thigh

On July 7, a casualty list containing the names of officers killed on July 1 appeared in The Evening Telegram.

The names of the dead, who were all from St. John's, included Lieutenant Hubert Herder, son of the newspaper's publisher, Captain Eric Ayre, Lieutenant Fred Mellor, Lieutenant Richard Shortall, Lieutenant Gerald Ayre, Lieutenant John Ferguson, and Lieutenant Wallace Ross.

Those reported missing included: Lieutenants Wilfrid Ayre, Robert Bruce Reid, Clifford Rendell and George Taylor.

On July 8, the paper reported that 230 Newfoundlanders had died at Beaumont Hamel on the first of July and published a long list of the dead and wounded.

Printed as well was the following poem, called For King and Country,

Far from their Island home they sleep
Under a foreign sun
Their only thought their country's call
And now, their life's work done.
O'er them we lay no mournful pall,
No requiem mass we sing.
In soldiers cloak our heroes lie
Serving, till death, their king,
No organ peals their funeral march
But bugle, drum and gun,
And lo, we hear a heavenly voice
"Well done, dear boys, well done.

The July 8 paper carried a message from King George to Field Marshal Haig saying how proud the king was of the troops, and offering congratulations on the recent fighting.

The same day, a letter from St. John's businessman S.O. Steele asked why Newfoundlanders couldn't get definite and immediate news of the Regiment's doings overseas. He said surely it could be arranged through the Pay and Records office to get press reports as soon as they were published, instead of having to wait for days.

Steele's son, Lieutenant Owen Steele, was killed July 7, the day before his father's letter appeared in the paper. Did the father know of his son's death when he wrote his letter? No one knows.

On July 10, The Evening Telegram announced that Sergeant Harold Mitchell and Sergeant Stan Newman, heroes of the Gallipoli Campaign, had arrived in Newfoundland on furlough.

In what was called "The Thrilling Story of the Opening of the Drive," writer Philip Gibbs, a correspondent of the London Daily Chronicle who was with the British armies in France, told the story of Beaumont Hamel with scarcely a mention of casualties.

The July 10 paper noted that German casualties to the end of June, 1916, were 3,013,637.

The paper's July 11 war news said only: "News of Somme battle continues entirely favourable."

There was, however, an item from London which hinted of what was to come: *Today's casualty list of British officers is the largest issued since the beginning of the offensive. It contains the names of 73 officers, many of whom belonged to the Newfoundland Contingent.*

It wasn't until July 13 that a full list of the casualties of July 1 became known to the people of Newfoundland. That day, in news from London, there was praise for the Newfoundland Regiment.

The Newfoundlanders were the only overseas troops engaged in these operations. The story of their heroic part cannot yet be told but when it is, it will make Newfoundland very proud. The Battalion pushed up to what may be called the third wave in the attack, probably the most formidable section of the whole of the German front, through an almost overwhelming artillery fire across the ground, which was swept by enfilading machine gun fire from hidden positions. The men behaved with completely noble steadiness and courage.

On July 14, The Evening Telegram went on the attack with an annoyed editorial that asked: *Are we rowing our weight in the boat?*

The editorial compared numbers of recruits from other colonies and said all but Newfoundland had sent a quota of seven per cent of the male population.

Based on those figures, it was reasoned that Newfoundland's contribution to the war effort should be 16,000 men, a significantly higher number than the 5,000 planned.

The editorial concluded with the stinging words:

Every name on the casualty list should have a corresponding name on the enlistment roll. If not, we are not rowing our weight in the boat.

On July 17, as if in response to the July 14 editorial, James Murphy had a poem in the paper which urged further enlistments in no uncertain terms:

> *O come on you slackers*
> *Now here is your chance*
> *To show your devotion*
> *You're wanted in France.*

❊

chapter seventeen

On July 6, what was left of the Newfoundland Regiment went back to Englebelmer where they were joined by 130 reinforcements. When the men returned to the trenches on July 14, taking over 450 yards of the front line east of Auchonvillers, they numbered a total of 271. [27]

On July 19, two full companies of 500 men, originally designated A and B Company, 3rd Battalion, but more often remembered as the 2nd A and B, left St. John's on board the Sicilian bound for Great Britain.

Six weeks later, the Sicilian again set sail from St. John's, this time with 242 reinforcements.

Newfoundland Governor Walter Davidson wrote Field Marshal Haig that he intended to maintain the 1st Newfoundland Battalion at war strength.

He told Haig too that the losses of July 1 at Beaumont Hamel had stimulated recruiting.

In March, April and May of 1916, more than 1,000 Newfoundlanders volunteered to serve overseas. In May, the Newfoundland government decided all new recruits had to sign up for the duration of the war and not, as had previously been the case, for a year.

By the end of 1916, there were a total of 2,210 enlistments, of whom 1,089 were accepted for service.

From Ayr, the 2nd (Reserve) Battalion at Ayr sent men across the Channel to France as soon as they were trained. By the end of 1916, the Newfoundland Regiment numbered more than 800 men. [28]

In Newfoundland, enlistment was influenced by individual recruiting by members of the Newfoundland Regiment who were home on leave recuperating from wounds.

Lieutenant George Hicks of Grand Falls, for example, came back from overseas with his arm in a sling. During October, his campaign for volunteers resulted in his signing up 270 new recruits.

Beaumont Hamel had wiped out almost all the Newfoundland Regiment's officers and specialists, including bombers, scouts, gunners, intelligence personnel, signalers, and snipers.

There was a rush now to commission officers and train specialists.

Potential officers were sent to an Officers Cadet unit for four months of training.

Future specialists were sent to schools of instruction, such as the School of Trench Warfare and Instruction to Hand Grenades at Troon. There was also a Machine Gun course at St. Andrews.

On July 17, the Newfoundland Regiment handed over their trenches to the South Wales Borderers and marched to Acheux for a short stay in billets.

On July 23, the Regiment and other units of the 88th Brigade, marched 10 miles westward to Beauval where they had a visit from Newfoundland Prime Minister, Sir Edward Morris.

The Newfoundlanders, by then up to a strength of 450 men, listened as Morris told them how proud the people of Newfoundland were of their Regiment, and how gratified they were at the splendid name Newfoundland soldiers had won for themselves and their country.

Morris told the troops that, even as he spoke, 550 men from Newfoundland were on their way to reinforce the ranks and help in the fray if they should ever again be called upon to go into action.

On his return to Newfoundland, Morris presented a report to Governor Davidson in which he spoke glowingly of the Newfoundland Regiment.

He went on to tell of visiting a French prisoner of war camp that held 1,000 Germans.

"It was a study to watch those men," he wrote. *"I never understood what the German machine meant till I saw them; there they were, no speculation in their eyes, sullen and sodden, moving around objectless and aimless, like animals in a zoo."*

From his musings on the German prisoners of war, Morris proceeded to comment on war in general.

"And why the war?" he asked. *"And what is all this for?*

After you have been to the Front and seen, and got right up against this indescribable horror of war through which the nations are now passing the question that is irresistibly borne in upon you is: Who is responsible for this titanic struggle? It is the greatest blunder of history."

On July 22, The Evening Telegram published a letter that Bert Ellis of Springdale Street had written to his mother from Wandsworth Hospital in London, England, on July 6.

Ellis had been wounded in the leg during the Battle of Beaumont Hamel, a battle he described as "like hell let loose."

He continued:

The Newfoundland Regiment is about done. They stood to their guns almost to the last man and fought like those who know no fear. When the roll was called only 43 answered.

When I was crawling back (for that's what puzzles me most-however I got back) I was all alone and never met a soul all the way back, which was 400 yards, only Dead! Dead! Everywhere.

The awful sight, it made me so sick that I used to lie down and wonder if would go on or stay there. It wouldn't have been so bad only they turned the guns on us as we were trying to get back.

Our boys acted throughout like heroes.

They went up on top singing just as if they were going on a march instead of facing death.

The place we went over, or just in front of us, was called the Happy Valley or the Vale of Death.

It put me in mind of Buckmaster's Field with the German trenches on LeMarchant Road and ours up on Adams Avenue, so when we came to the skyline they just mowed us down. But our own boys showed no fear.

Ellis ended his letter: *Love to all the family. We will have victory soon.*

On July 22, there was news that more than 200,000 French and British troops had attacked the German lines north and south of the Somme on a front of 27 miles.

On July 27 an editorial stated: *It has been a sad month for Newfoundland and the long interval of silence that followed the list of officers killed added greatly to the anxiety of all.* ✸

In Flanders Fields
In Flanders fields the poppies blow
Between the crosses, row on row
That mark our place; and in the sky
The larks, still bravely singing, fly
Scarce heard amid the guns below.

We are the Dead. Short days ago
We lived, felt dawn, saw sunset glow,
Loved and were loved, and now we lie
In Flanders fields.

Take up our quarrel with the foe:
To you from failing hands we throw
The torch; be yours to hold it high.
If ye break faith with us who die
We shall not sleep, though poppies grow
In Flanders fields.

John McCrae (1872-1918)

 chapter eighteen

The Battle of the Somme, which had its beginning on July 1, 1916, would continue until the third week of November, with the major share of the conflict carried out by the British Fourth and Fifth Armies.

From July to November, General Haig's three armies, the Third, First and Second, held the long front from Gommecourt to Boesinghe, five miles north of Ypres, in west Flanders.

The 29th Division, which included the Newfoundland Regiment, was part of the Second Army.

In comparison to the main battle area, the front held by Haig's armies was a quiet area where the troops primary role was to maintain constant pressure against the enemy, to furnish the main offensive with fresh divisions, and to supply materials needed at the Front.

Towards the end of July, the Newfoundland Regiment crossed the Belgian border to Poperinghe, where they had two nights in billets before being sent to hold a sector of the front line in Ypres.

The Ypres Salient was a deep curve that measured 17 miles, from Steenstraat, north of Ypres, to Saint-Eloi, to the south.

Across its eight-mile base ran the Yser Canal, which constricted movement in and out of the area. Ypres had once been the heart of the flourishing Flanders cloth industry, as represented by the massive Gothic style Cloth Hall that overlooked the town's main square. All roads in the vicinity of Ypres passed through the town like spokes on a wheel.

The Germans, on the high ground around Passchendaele, six miles northeast of Ypres, had an almost clear view of the entire area, and with their guns ranged on three sides could shell it from three directions with ease.

When the Newfoundlanders arrived in Ypres, they were given accommodation in dugouts and cellars. Not far from where C Company was staying in the cellar of a reform school was the infamous Hellfire Corner. A crossroads on the Menin Road which was under constant German observation and where any movement set off a flurry of enemy shells, Hellfire Corner was said to be the most dangerous spot on the Flemish front.

Throughout the war, Ypres itself was under constant attack as the key point of an Allied defense line that blocked a German approach to the English Channel.

The first Battle of Ypres took place from October 30 to November 24, 1914, when outnumbered British, French and Belgian troops resisted a German offensive aimed at the English Channel.

The offensive, which was potentially disastrous to the Allied cause, was stemmed after 34 days of fighting and resulted in fixed military positions, initiating the long period of trench warfare on the Western Front.

The second Battle of Ypres lasted from April 22 to May 25, 1915, and resulted in Allied casualties of approximately 60,000 and German losses of about 35,000.

It was at the Second Battle of Ypres that Canadian troops had their baptism of fire.

From Salisbury Plain in England, the Canadians had been sent to France in February and then on to Hazebrouck, in French Flanders, where they were billeted in nearby villages and farms.

On April 22, 1915, the Canadians were in the front lines, four miles northeast of Ypres, in Flanders Fields, when the Germans released 5,730 cylinders of chlorine gas.

The poisonous gas rolled in an olive green vapour over the Allied trenches. Without gas masks, without protection of any kind, 5,000 men, their lungs seared and burning, choked and died. Thousands of others fled in terror.

The result was an unexpected four-mile gap in the Allied defenses.

The surprised Germans, who had no idea of the effect their powerful new weapon would have, didn't have enough manpower to take advantage of the breach in the Allied line.

After an advance of two miles, the Germans dug in, deciding to wait until morning for the arrival of fresh troops and supplies, before proceeding on to Ypres.

There are some who believe if the Germans had not waited, if they had pushed on to Ypres, they might have been able to encircle 50,000 British and Canadian troops and win a tremendous victory. If the surprise of poison gas had been correctly exploited, the result might well have been the enemy breaking the trench deadlock and winning the war in the West.

At the second Battle of Ypres, Lance Corporal Frederick Fisher of the 13th Battalion, who held the Germans away from Canadian guns, won Canada's first Victoria Cross of the war.

The novice Canadian troops received high praise for holding the line until British reinforcements arrived late on the evening of April 24 but the price paid was steep, more than 6,000 Canadians were killed and wounded.

The British Army, including the Canadians, lost nearly 60,000 men in the second Battle of Ypres. The carnage wrought near Ypres prompted Major John McCrae, a Canadian surgeon who was there, to write his famous poem: "In Flanders Fields the poppies blow. Between the crosses row on row..."

When the Newfoundland Regiment arrived in Ypres in late July of 1916, they went into brigade reserve on the east side of the town and were soon hard at work building, repairing and fortifying trenches which had been badly damaged in earlier fighting.

Persistent enemy bombardment with shrapnel shells, called whizz-bangs or whistling Willies by the men, kept flattening the parapets, which needed constant rebuilding. Barbed wire in front also had to be frequently strengthened.

Death was a constant companion in the trenches.

Aside from shrapnel shells, there were high explosives, dubbed Black Marias, Jack Johnsons or coal boxes; and trench mortars (minenwerfer) which lobbed projectiles shaped like small rum bottles. Whatever the name, the exploding shells caused terrible, often untreatable injuries, beheading and maiming unfortunate victims with jagged pieces of steel, or burying them beneath tons of dirt. Artillery was an around-the-clock threat with possibly two-thirds of all casualties caused by big guns. And then there were deadly snipers who picked men off whenever they got a chance.

On the night of August 8, the Germans followed up a heavy bombardment by launching a gas attack. It was the first time the Newfoundlanders had been subjected to cloud gas, although they had previously experienced poison gas from exploding shells.

Nicholson, in The Fighting Newfoundlanders, says the fact the Newfoundlanders did not sustain a single casualty in this attack speaks well for the quality of their anti-gas training. Neighbouring units had as many as 300 gassed, not from being caught without their gas helmets, but from taking them off too soon, as well as from re-entering dugouts before they had been decontaminated.

Toxic chemical agents, popularly called poison gases, were first used in World War I when the French fired rifle grenades filled with tear gas in battle in November, 1914.

The Germans fired several shells filled with liquid chlorine in Poland in January, 1915, but the chlorine failed to volatilize in the intense cold.

In April, 1915, Germans released chlorine gas from cylinders, killing 5,000 in the second Battle of Ypres. Six months later, the British retaliated with a chlorine gas attack at Loos.

A total of 32 chemical agents were used during the First World War, but only 12 proved practical and effective. Included among them were lung irritants or choking agents such as chlorine, and blister gases such as mustard.

As a result of gas warfare, gas masks, chlorine-filled artillery shells and other items of chemical warfare were rapidly developed. The Newfoundland Regiment's Dr. Cluny MacPherson is credited with designing one of the earliest prototypes of the gas mask.

A St. John's man, MacPherson enlisted in the Regiment in 1914 with the rank of Captain and went overseas in March 1915 as principal medical officer. The use of poison gas by the Germans, and MacPherson's ideas on protection led to a tour of front line positions and hospitals in France, and membership on the first war office committee on Poison Gas Protection.

In July 1915, anticipating that Turkey might use poison gas, MacPherson was transferred to Gallipoli. Later that same year he saw service in Italy and Egypt. After being injured in Egypt, he was invalided back to Newfoundland and served as Director of Medical Services for the Militia. He was demobilized in 1919 with the rank of Lieutenant Colonel. [29]

Jim Stacey was well aware of poison gas when he arrived in the Ypres Salient in late July, 1916.

Belgium - The Ypres Salient

Reinforcements were arriving and this meant that we would soon be up to full strength. At the same time we were on the move once again and headed for Belgium. We arrived on the Ypres Salient at the end of July. It was here that the Germans had first sent poison gas over on the Canadians in 1915. Our side was using it when we arrived. It was contained in pressurized canisters tucked under the front line trench with rubber hoses connected to the containers. The hoses led out over our parapet like fingers from a glove. I suppose the Germans had the same arrangements on their side. A sentry would be posted guard, alongside a compressed air canister with a horn attached. He would be specifically assigned to sound the alarm when the enemy released poison gas. Just turning the cock could turn on the alarm and the release of the compressed air would trigger the horn. That would be warning enough, as the poison gas released would need a nine-mile an hour wind to take it across no-mans-land to our trench. There were painted signs everywhere - on one side, "gas alarm on", on the other side, "gas alarm off". When "off", the wind was usually blowing in our favour. The sentry would also have to watch a cross-stuck in the ground with two pieces of twine attached and cotton wool tied on the end. This would let him know from which direction the wind was blowing. He also had to listen for a hissing noise as gas escaped from the hose. Very often the sentry gave a false alarm.

When in supports, in Ypres, we stayed in billets known as the Ramparts. In these billets we had wire netting bunks. The rats were numerous and every night they would be around. When you were sleeping, you did not mind them because you could not hear them. There was one rat that had a cold and used to sniffle. One minute you could hear him on the other side of the room and the next minute he would be under the bunk. It was impossible to get any sleep because of the noise he made. I thought of a plan to keep him out. I found a hole where he entered and placed a part of a loaf of bread near it so he would have his hunger satisfied and go away (not coming back to disturb my rest) The plan worked.

Belgium was in low fen country so we could not dig trenches. We used sand-bags filled with clay to build and make our trenches and parapets. To the right of the salient there were no man-made trenches, but a blank of no-mans-land, which was covered by machine gun posts dug under the railway track. At night a listening patrol was in front; behind were five bombing posts evenly spaced across to the trenches on the other side. This was a weak spot in the line and we expected that if the Germans made an attack it would be spearheaded here; therefore, we were always on the alert.

Captain Raley took me with rifle and bandoleer to visit the bombing posts one night. Reporting to Capt. March of "D" Company we procured a guide whom took us to No. 1 post, then a guide from No.1 took us to No.2 and so on. It was a clear night with lights from both sides lighting up the area. We had to stand still when their flares came over because of an occasional burst of machine gun fire. We had just reached No.3 post when the gas alarm horn was sounded. Then all horns along the line sounded. I immediately sat down and put on my pH gas helmet. It was a false alarm as the wind was blowing toward the German line.

Our guns opened up on this piece of no-mans-land; then the enemy opened up. With flares on both sides it was as light as day. We took off our gas masks and with a hundred-yard dash we reached the trenches on the other side, just on the outside of Y wood (or what was left of it). It was a tangle of fallen trees, shell holes and barbed wire. Here we found the Lincoln Regiment still with *their gas masks on. The shellfire looked as if hell had let loose. The Menin Ypres Road was on the other side of the Y Wood, which we made for. Raley was ahead. A tree had fallen across the road, which I supposed Raley did not see as he tripped and fell down losing his helmet. Here we were raked with our own machine gun fire. As we lay on the road, a shell burst overhead. Something struck my right foot that felt like a sledgehammer. Losing all feeling in my foot I felt it to see if it was still there. I told Raley I was hit and he told me to get on his back, but instead I crawled in the ditch and waited until the shelling had subsided. Then I made a run down the road forgetting I was wounded. I found out afterwards that a shrapnel ball had penetrated the sole of my boot and ended up at my toes.*

While we were holding the Ypres Salient, approximately a dozen carrier pigeons were put in my care. They would be used if we were surrounded and all other means of communications were cut off. They were in a cage and had to be fed very sparingly with the grain that was sent with them. Raley sent them back because they were not needed. Attached to one of the pigeon's legs was a capsule in which a coded message on very fine paper could be placed. They could not be kept longer than three days. When let loose they would return to the pigeon farms that was at General Headquarters, a safe distance behind the line. There the messages were taken off their legs, decoded and relayed to the appropriate destination. In the German advance of March 1918, they passed our pigeon farm, so every bird had to be killed; otherwise the enemy could use them to their advantage.

Poperinghe, a fair size town, was about twelve kilometres from Ypres. There were a few shops and cafes still open. When in supports at Ypres, I often took a walk down there. I have a photo that was taken there (which I treasure) of Bill Eaton, Walter Thistle and myself. We could get a fairly good meal there. Another spot was "Hell Fire Corner", a place that was aptly named and never to be forgotten by the troops who held the salient. Not too far from it was the Horn works, which was held by "D" Company and commanded by Capt. March. "C" Company commanded by Capt. Donnelly was in the school while "A" and "B" Companies were in Ypres, North of the Horn Works.

Hellfire Corner was a simple crossroads on the Menin (Menen) Road. A light Railway also crossed the road at this point in those days, passing across the fields to Railway Wood. The position was therefore accurately marked on all maps of the area and the German artillery, on slightly higher ground to the East, could shell it accurately at any time, day or night.

On October 5, the Newfoundland Regiment was sent to Poperinghe for a three-night break before heading back to the Somme, where the grim struggle was continuing.

During the time the Newfoundlanders were at Ypres, the Fourth Army had, after three months of fighting, inched its way forward four and a half miles.

At the end of September, General Haig called for an offensive to be launched October 12 which was intended to push the whole line forward an average of two miles from Le Transloy and Beaulencourt, across the valley of the upper Ancre to Gommecourt. This would be the 10th of 12 battles that make up the Battle of the Somme, and it was named the Battle of Transloy Ridge, after a spur covering the villages of Le Transloy and Beaulencourt.

It was to this battle that the Newfoundlanders, with the 88th Brigade, were now committed.

On October 8, the Newfoundlanders arrived in Longeau, a small station near Amiens. A march of eight miles brought them to Corbie, at the junction of the Ancre River with the Somme.

At Corbie, the Regiment settled into billets, only to learn the next day they had to go into the line on the night of October 10. By 9:30 the following evening, the troops were manning a 500-yard firing line on the northern outskirts of Gueudecourt.

The 88th Brigade was given two successive objectives called the Green Line and the Brown Line. The Green Line involved the capture of a portion of the German defenses known as Hilt Trench, about 400 yards from the British position on the northern outskirts of Gueudecourt.

The Brown Line was about 400 yards further on.

A new form of tactics had been devised for this offensive, which involved close co-operation between advancing infantry and support artillery.

In what was called "the creeping barrage" the artillery was to put down a curtain of shrapnel fire just ahead of the attacking lines. The guns shifted their fire forward at a rate of about 50 yards each minute and the infantry were ordered to keep not more than 50 yards behind it.

The advantage of the creeping barrage was that the Germans were compelled to stay under cover and had no time to bring their machine guns into action. The disadvantage was that any deviation could result in troops being hit by their own shellfire.

Using the creeping barrage, the Newfoundlanders captured Hilt Trench and had the distinction of being one of the few units in the whole of the Fourth Army Front to capture and retain its objective.

The Newfoundland Regiment's success at Gueudecourt did not come cheap. From the time they went into the trenches on October 10, until they were relieved 53 hours later, there were 239 casualties, of which 120 were fatal.

Captain James Donnelly, who had won a Military Cross at Caribou Hill in Suvla Bay, was among those killed at Gueudecourt. Three Newfoundlanders were awarded the Distinguished Conduct Medal for their gallantry on October 12: Sergeant-Major Cyril Gardner of British Harbour, Trinity Bay; Sergeant Peter Samson of Fox Harbour, Placentia

Bay; and Lance-Corporal William Bennett of Stephenville.

Captain Wesley March was awarded a Military Cross for his courage and skill in leading the initial attack.

For personally killing 15 Germans, Captain Bert Butler added a bar to the Military Cross he'd received for his part in night raids prior to the Battle of Beaumont Hamel .

The farthest point reached by the Regiment on October 12, 1916, is marked by a bronze caribou, similar to one at Beaumont Hamel. [30] ⚙

Regiment moves through Berneville on horseback, bicycle and on foot after the fighting at Monchy Le Preux and Les Fosses Farm 1917 (courtesy The Trail of the Caribou)

 chapter nineteen

On the last day of October the Newfoundland Regiment, together with other battalions of the 88th Brigade, marched to the village of Ville-sur-Ancre, remembered by the Newfoundlanders as Ville. The men spent two weeks in billets in Ville, and it was here that Captain Tom Nangle came to the Regiment as Roman Catholic chaplain.

Shortly before leaving St. John's, the popular Father Nangle had been the recipient of a " purse of gold and an illuminated address" during a farewell dinner held at the O' Donel wing of the Benevolent Irish Society hall.

Jim Stacey wrote about Gueudecourt, and the later arrival of the new padre.

Gueudecourt

Our stay in Ypres came to an end on October 10th, when we boarded buses to take us to Corbie on the Somme. From there we moved up in front of Gueudecourt, where the 12th Division went over the top in late September and concluded a successful operation. We came out of the line to Switch Trench (why it was called "Switch", I do not know). We found out that there were three dugouts of galvanized iron, which were taken by Officers. Dr. Bower who had come from the 87th Brigade to replace Dr. Rocher who was on leave took one. There was no shelter for the others, so they had to set about getting shelters the best way they could, with any materials they could lay their hands on, which was not much. Some rigged up shelters in the trenches, which at the time were dry, a condition that would not last.

Eaton, Thistle and I salvaged three rubber sheets and dug the top off the trench so that the three of us could stretch out to sleep. We anchored the rubber sheets so that if it rained we would stay dry. Just after that the rain came and because there was no drainage the water half filled the trench and those there had to get to higher ground. Being on top, we did not fare too badly. The water bent the sheets down in the centre where there happened to be a small hole. We had to watch it so that when the water reached the hole we pushed up from the inside to overflow it safely away from us. In the trench there was mud everywhere and at night when we turned in, our boots and puttees were covered with it. We went down to Army Service Corps and procured empty sandbags that were just long and wide enough to tie on each leg up to the knee. We put them on before going to bed, if you call it bed. We soon found out that these bags were a great cure for cold and wet feet. You had to sleep with your head alongside your buddy's feet and we sometimes felt like sardines in a tin. After a while the rain changed to frost, as the weather became colder. It became unbearable in the trenches.

We were not out of shell range and an occasional one was dropped on us. On one particular night we had just turned in and the candle was still alight, when Fritz sent one over. It was so close that it put the candle out and exploded not too far away. "That was a close one", someone said, to which we all agreed and gave it no more thought. It was just getting daylight when the Sergeant Major pulled back the rubber sheet that closed the entrance and said, "Get a move on and give a hand to dig out the Doctor." The Doctor's galvanized iron dugout lined on the outside with sandbags collapsed when the shell struck the top and buried him alive. If the policeman on duty had not vacated his post when the shell came over and had gotten help to dig the Doctor out, there would have been a good chance to save him. He was with the Regiment only two days. We dug a grave and Mike Smyth conducted the burial service with the singing of the hymn "Nearer my God to Thee". As a gravestone, a rifle was stuck barrel down in the ground and on the butt we carved his name. Eaton took his personal possessions, as they had to be sent to General Headquarters. There was a letter he had received two days before from his wife in England. In it she said how lucky he had been to be sent to France, because the ship he was supposed to travel on to Mesopotamia was torpedoed with a loss of all hands (such is war).

It was on the same day that we moved back through the communications trench that was called, "Cocoa Alley". This was the most bitterly fought for piece of ground on the Somme. It was not uncommon to see a man's arm or foot pressing against the wire, which held the sides of the trench in place. We stayed at Bernefly Wood for a rest in the mud, amid a battery of 9.2 inch Naval Guns. It was here that Pioneer Sgt. Pitcher made a cross for Dr Bower's grave and he took it back to replace the rifle.

The battery consisted of three 9.2-inch guns. They were in action very often; so much so, that they caused a lot of discomfort to the signalers who were sending and receiving messages by Morse code. I observed one chap trying to receive a message by candlelight. Just as he was all set to take down the message, "Bang", went number one gun and out would go the candle. He would set the candle alight again and just as he was all set to take the message down again, "Bang", would go number two, and so on with Number three. It was a while before that message was taken.

Now the frosty season was setting in; light frost made the mud worse. To be dry and comfortable was out of the question. We were sleeping or resting on a rubber sheet over wet mud. Being called in the night to take a message and having only one pair of dry socks, there was only one thing to do - that is take off the dry socks and put on the wet ones, then set out to deliver the message. By doing so in the dark, you might step into a mud hole up to your knees. When you returned, you could take off the wet socks, put on the dry ones and then get under the blanket.

The time came to move back to the Gueudecourt sector. Headquarters was at Bull Trench just over the ridge from Gueudecourt. The Battalion went in the line from Bull Trench. The ground rose and dipped on the other side. There were three disabled tanks that acted as a landmark; these were the first types to be used in the war, they had a wheel in front that was used for steering. If the wheel, which must have been a special target, was broken, then the tank could not move and consequently became a sitting duck. By all appearances these three had encountered this problem. Bull Trench was unhealthy in more ways than shellfire as the German dead had not been buried after a recent advance. While we were sitting around in our dugouts eating our dinner, someone brought our attention to the ground. When we jumped on it, it shook like jelly. We investigated and found a dead German under the topsoil.

During the winter you would not put in any more than two days at a time on the front line which at times consisted of shell holes. One night when we were getting relieved, the guides for the Battalion relieving us, came to Battalion Headquarters and we sent our own guides back with them to show them the way, so that there would be less confusion during the night in taking over the respective Companies. The guides of the two Regiments were going up the line when a shell pitched in the middle of them, killing some, wounding and shell-shocking others.

I was now put in charge of the runners and guides and had to get substitutes as the units came to Headquarters. Having guided three units that day, I was now very tired and substitutes were used who did not know the way.

Herb Vaughn, one of the guides I did not know at the time, came into my restaurant in St. John's after the war with some friends. He introduced me by pointing his finger at saying, and me "He nearly got me shot". Then he went on to say that he was one of the substitute guides I had sent with a Unit of Australians to take up to the line that night. Of course, he did not know where he was going in the dark so he stopped and said he was lost. The officer in charge (so he said) put a gun to his head and accused him of being a spy.

I will never forget the next morning when, in broad daylight, Capt. March came over the rise with his men; they were late getting relieved. We, at Headquarters, stood by expecting the enemy to open fire at any moment as they passed by the three disabled tanks, but not a shot was heard.

I was put in charge of the Battalion Runners when Walter Thistle was wounded. I was also given the responsibility for six bicycles, which were made to fold up when being transported. Before I knew it one of the bikes was missing. In good faith I reported it to the CO and he accused me of stealing it. My mind went back to a time in Suez when we had kit inspection. I was minus a cartridge pouch and was charged 4/11 for it and it was taken off my pay. It dawned on me that I might also have to pay for the missing bicycle, so I replaced it the same way, by waiting outside the canteen until I saw someone leave his bike to go in and make a purchase. To my knowledge, everyone did the same. I jumped on the bike and rode off with it. At one time I had as many as nine bikes, six in operation and three being repaired at the Division Armory. This method of procuring missing things in the Army seemed to be an established fact. Col. Hadow, who I visited at Kent, England, told me that the Transport Officer, Stan Goodyear, did the same. Often in the night he had taken a horse from another Battalion's transport lines and smeared the identifying colour marks with paint.

We were in this area for the remainder of the 1916-17 winter. The ground was so ploughed up by shellfire you couldn't tell that villages had been there, except for the bricks or pieces of iron railing scattered about. All the trees were shattered and even to find a piece of burnable wood was almost impossible. The roads were very soft and muddy and they could not stand up to the steady use of the Army Transport. There were gangs of men continually scraping off mud and covering the surface with gravel. The gravel, however, would soon disappear into the mud. It was difficult even to walk along the sides of the roads because of the mud. If you left the road to go up the line to the trenches you would have to use duck boards. Duckboards consisted of two 2x4 planks evenly nailed across with four feet long scantlings with spaces equidistant between each of them. They would take you over the mud and shell holes. We used braziers for heating. A brazier consisted of a large tin can with holes punched in the sides. We would use them in our dugouts. We normally used charcoal as a fuel, but that was largely unobtainable, so we would use wood when it could be found. The smokestack was usually the entrance to the dugout. The saying was, "It was better to have warm smoke than damp fog".

We found it was better to lay on the floor or as near as possible to it so that we would not choke on the smoke. The smoke also made our eyes smart. We also had to be careful of the smoke because it could become a target for the Germans. We also had Canned Heat. It was given to those in the front line or other exposed posts. We were generally twenty-four hours in the front line and forty-eight hours in supports. Some parts of the front line were nothing but shell holes and you were forced to lie down all day and would not dare show yourself. On these occasions we used Canned Heat to heat our meals and keep warm. While here we could not make a fire to cook, so hot soup was sent up in vacuum containers strapped to fit snugly on the back like a pack.

When we returned to the trenches after a rest we usually moved to the right of the section we originally departed from. On one occasion when we returned, we moved to an area that was just behind the le Transloy Summer Trench. There had been an advance here just before we took over. To guide us from the back area, at night, were pieces of white tape attached to sticks pushed into the ground. These sticks very often went missing as they would get knocked down or covered with mud. To guide us, by day, the most visible landmark was a plane that had been shot down. I would use it to find Battalion Headquarters, which was just over the rise. We could always manage to find our way in daylight but at night it was hopeless.

The "Jack Johnson" High Explosive shells would come over and bury themselves in the soft wet ground, then burst. If they struck an area close to where you were standing you would get a shower of mud, sods or anything else that was movable. I sent two runners on a message - always two at a time in this area to Brigade Headquarters just before dark. At midnight they had not returned so I reported to Col. Hadow. He said, "I am not surprised, I got lost myself". They arrived back at daylight. They did get lost and they stayed in a trench for the night. Hadow and I were out before dawn visiting what was our front line, shell holes half filled with water. Through the haze we saw a squad of men walking in No-Man's-Land toward the German line and put them on the right track.

It was on that very night that we were being relieved. The Regiment had already left and a guide was sent from Transport to take us back. Battalion Headquarters was always the last to leave. There were about a dozen in all: Hadow, Raley, Dr. Tocher, the Runners, the Red Cross and the signalers. Before leaving and knowing that there was a lot of mud to go through, I wrapped a pair of sand bags around my legs to keep my puttees dry and clean. We left about midnight starting down the sunken road toward the village of Les Boeufs .Dr. Tocher wore glasses and even then his eyesight was not very good. We noticed he was walking into the shell holes half-filled with water. When we left he had a stick and was wearing his glasses and now they were both gone. So, I took one of his arms and Lionel Munn, another runner, took his other arm and we pushed and pulled the doctor around the shell holes. As we were going down the sunken road, we veered to the left just as the shells came over. We could also see German flares. Hadow halted us and said we were going toward the German line; he and Raley huddled in the ditch alongside and took out his trench map, flashlight and compass. Yes, we were going towards the German line. I still think the guide was on the right track. There was a bend in the road further on that would have veered to the right toward the village of Flers, Hadow stood there and sent out individuals within hearing distance of each other to scout around while others went out beyond but kept contact. They discovered a trench with troops in it, so we connected up with them and went the rest of the way on the duckboards. Hadow was cool and did not in any way criticize the Transport guide.

We finally reached the Battalion at Trones wood. What grieved me most during this episode was that these troops had a canteen where coffee was sold but because we did not belong to their Division, the guards would not sell or give us any. While eating I took the muddy sandbags off my legs and my puttees were clean. Hadow wanted to know how I kept them so clean so I told him. After a short rest we moved up to the front line and found ourselves at Sailly-Saillisel. Here the Regiment met considerable resistance. We had another short rest, then moving along we passed Ginchy Corner or crossroads which everyone dreaded. The German gunners had the road marked and would fire spontaneously, and you never knew until they sent over another salvo. As we were passing along, we saw a number of limbers in the ditch. I looked over on the other side of the road and saw about a dozen laid out with rubber sheets over them. We marched along and came in contact with some more shooting. This was a different kind, there was a movie camera set up on a high section of ground and an operator was winding away. I never gave it another thought until the C.B.C. showed a film taken during World War I of the Regiment going up the line. They announced that they had procured it from the British War Archives. It had the appearance of being taken on the Somme battlefield and no doubt this was the one taken on the road past Ginchy Corner.

I think the worst place we held the line was at Combles. Winter was approaching fast and there was mud everywhere. Everything had to be carried on our backs up the line, even hot soup was carried in containers. One could stand no more than twenty-four hours in the line at any one time. When we were relieved, we were billeted for a while in a small village called {Cosy or Carnoy. The orderly room was in the front room of a farmhouse and Stan Goodyear, Transportation Officer, had a bedroom there. The house and barn were laid out in the usual French style - a square with the barn beside it and the house fitted in at the top from the roadside. A pile of manure was situated in the centre at the front and lay between them. Close to the front door, there was a well covered with a saddle roof and a windlass using a chain with a bucket attached. The door to the orderly room opened close to the well. The orderly room staff and other ranks slept in the upstairs of the barn close to the house. There were several four-bushel sacks that we used for beds. The roof formed an apex, with gutters at the eaves to collect rainwater, which I later *found out ran by pipe into the well. We arranged with Madame to pool our rations. She would supply eggs and other tid-bits and allows the use of her stove. We would supply other items such as bacon. Each one of the staff would get up in his turn to get breakfast. One morning, Bill Eaton, the Sergeant clerk, was up and about getting his breakfast. One would hardly expect a toilet or bathroom to be in a barn, so we used a large fruit tin for emergencies. I had just such an emergency and used the tin this particular morning. There was an open window in the centre of the roof. I emptied the contents of the tin on to the roof from this window. As I did so I saw Eaton and Madame, by the door, close to the well, talking. It was one of those still mornings, with no wind, I heard the fluid run down the gutter and into the well and to my horror. Madame heard it too and pointed her finger to the window where I was standing. Whatever she said fully convinced Eaton that I was the offender.*

November was drawing to a close. We moved further back to the village of Champs-en-Amienois, which was about twelve miles from the town of Amiens. Here we were to spend a month, which included Christmas. The orderly room was in Madame Auchelon's house and our sleeping quarters were in the barn alongside. We slept in the loft amongst the hay. We had a grand time here. Madame would even bring us coffee in the mornings. There was Edward Popaleon, a hired man, garcon the boy and Madame. The village soon began to have the appearance of St John's. The roads had signs painted with names such as Water Street, LeMarchant Road and so on. As Christmas came nearer, we, the orderly room staff, four runners and two clerks, planned to celebrate the season with a dinner in the orderly room and invite Madame, Edward Popaleon and Garcon. We had to scrounge around to see what we could get for Madame to cook. She sold us the chicken, which I killed with an axe, and cabbage, but we had to procure the rest where we could. We had lots of Christmas pudding and several varieties of refreshments: a good supply of S.R.D. (army rum), vin blanc, and vin rouge and citron champagne. We tried to get Edward to drink the rum so we could get him drunk, but he was too cute. He would drink all the champagne we would give him with no effect, which cost five francs a bottle, whereas the rum was free. I have a photo of some of the boys that was taken at the time. For decorations we used mistletoe. There were many apple trees on the sides of the road and mistletoe, being a parasite, grew on those trees. When the leaves were gone it was readily available.

Our good holiday came to a close after Christmas and we were off again to the sea of mud. Meaulte was the village where we stopped, it was just outside our original line, where we had been shortly before July 1st. We were billeted in a barn, identical to all others on the farms around the area. The farmer and his wife lived in the house. When we arrived, someone asked them for a drink of water, which they refused to give. They were not very friendly. There was a pigeon cote attached to the gable of the barn across from us. It had a shutter that could be closed or opened with a line. In the evening, just about dusk, the farm lady came out and closed the door, sure that all the pigeons were inside. When she left, we discovered that there was one pigeon left out, so I went and told the lady about it and asked if we could open the shutter and let it in. She said, "No", as all the rest would "Party". Just after that, Sgt. Charlie Parsons of the Signal Corps came along. We drew his attention to the lone pigeon trying to get in the cote and we said, "Charlie pull the string and let the poor creature in". As the lady said, all the pigeons flew out. At the same time the farmer came out from his house with a gun in his hand. Charlie turned white with fright and we all disappeared into our billets in a hurry and closed the door.

While here, Padre Nangle joined us after coming back off leave. In the meantime Reverend Stenlake had taken his place as Padre. His job was to cater to the Officer's Mess in which he had to buy all extras for the Mess as well as keeping track of the issued rations. Also in his care were all the refreshments including the alcoholic beverages. It was late in the evening when Padre Nangle arrived and Padre Stenlake was in bed. There he was with a case of whiskey at his head for safety and a bag of prayer books at his feet. Padre Nagle remarked smiling, "I don't know what religion is coming to, a clergyman has a case of whiskey under his head and a bag of prayer books at his feet".

We were on the move again, back to the Somme mud. Maj. Forbes Robertson took command when our CO, Col. Hadow , went on leave for over four months. He told me when I visited him that no one could stand any more than six months at a time, in a theatre of war.

It was on November 24th that I was granted leave myself. I had ten days leave to England (Blighty). The first place I went was to the Pay and Records office on Victoria St. London. There I presented my pay book to receive my back pay, which amounted to sixty-nine pounds. After receiving this amount I was in clover. The first thing in my mind was to go to an outfitter's and get a whole outfit from the crown of my head to the soles of my feet. I took the outfit with me, had a bath, then dumped my take-offs in the corner and put on the new, which was the best that money could buy. By so doing I could get rid of all my bosom friends. A ten-day leave after twelve months continuous active service without a break was heavenly. I could walk the streets of London or anywhere with the Somme mud on my boots and puttees with pride and feel inwardly that I was doing my bit. I had made an allotment of eighty cents a day of my pay to a current account of the Bank of Montreal, London. I received a chequebook with this, which came in handy later, on when fifteen francs were not enough. During leave I went home, of course, but with only ten days I was afraid to go far. I returned back to the Somme mud after my ten days expired.

On November 17, the Newfoundlanders and the Worcesters took over front line positions north east of the village of Lesboeufs. On December

9, they were relieved in the front line and began a month in reserve, with stays in Meaulte, Mericourt-l'Abbe, Fricourt, Carnoy, Conde and Camps-en-Amienois.

As Christmas approached, there was an opportunity for members of the Regiment who had been six months or more in France to take leave in London.

The final Battle of the Somme, the Battle of the Ancre, ended on November 19, 1916.

The high point of the offensive was the British seizing of the Y Ravine and the ruins of Beaumont Hamel. The victory was the outcome of practically five months' flanking operations in which upwards of fifty divisions took part, most of them more than once.

The capture included 1,200 German prisoners who were taken out of deep dugouts in the Y Ravine, as well as a plentiful stock of provisions, including canned meats, sardines, cigars and thousands of bottles of beer.

In marked contrast, as pointed out by one historian, "the ground over which the advance was made was still littered with the skeletons clad in rags which represented the men who had fallen in the attack of July 1." [31]

The Battle of Ancre was the last of 12 battles that are collectively referred to as the Battle of the Somme. The casualty figures for the entire five month offensive are astounding. British and French casualties were about 600,000. The Germans lost equally as many soldiers. The total number of casualties was a mind-boggling total of 1,200,000 individuals.

For the men of the Newfoundland Regiment, the remaining days of 1916, and practically all of the first month of 1917 were spent in rest camps. This was the period of reconstruction, and of preparation for the severe battles of the following spring. ⊛

▓ *chapter twenty*

The year 1917 began with the Allies determined to take the initiative on the Western Front and be prepared to launch general offensives with all they had.

On January 11, the Newfoundland Regiment left Camps-en-Amienois.

The 29th Division, to which they were attached, was now responsible for a front, extending 1,000 yards north of Sailly-Saillisel to 1,000 yards northeast of Lesboeufs. On January 24, the Newfoundlanders took over a section of this front in readiness for a well-rehearsed surprise attack on the enemy. The operation was one of three secondary attacks planned by General Rawlinson in keeping with Haig's orders to make the enemy believe that the Battle of the Somme was starting again.

The day chosen for the offensive was January 27, the birthday of German Kaiser William.

At 5:30 a.m. a bombardment by the artillery of five divisions opened the attack.

Advancing behind the barrage, the 1st Royal Inniskilling Fusiliers and the 1st Border Regiment successfully gained their objective, 1,000 yards of the German first and second line of trenches.

On the day of battle, a total of 368 German prisoners were taken, with 72 captured by a single soldier of the Newfoundland Regiment, Sergeant Major Cyril Gardner.

After taking part in the early morning bombardment, the Regiment's C Company was assigned the task of helping to bring in the wounded and carry forward any equipment needed.

Gardner was in No Man's Land helping to pick up wounded when, alone and unarmed, he found himself face to face with a trench full of Germans. One of the Germans quickly put up his hands and the fast thinking Gardner quickly grabbed his revolver and somehow made it be known that everyone else on the enemy side had surrendered and they were the only ones left.

On getting the drift of what he was saying, the Germans gave up, and Gardner began marching his 72 prisoners back to his own line.

Enroute across No Man's Land, he was challenged by a British officer, who would have fired on the Germans if Gardner hadn't stopped him. Among the captured Germans was an officer who, realizing that the Newfoundlander had likely saved his life, removed the Iron Cross from his own chest and pinned it to Gardner's. His own country awarded Gardner a Bar to the Distinguished Conduct Medal which he had previously won in Gueudecourt.

Another hero of the day was Lieutenant Bert Holloway, the Regiment's Intelligence Officer,

With a few men, Holloway made his way across No Man's Land immediately after the initial bombardment. He went more than a mile behind the German Front Line and brought back useful intelligence information as well as six captured Germans.

In this action, the Newfoundland Regiment suffered several casualties, including seven killed,

By February 13, newly promoted Field-Marshal Haig had taken over more of the French front.

The Fourth Army's right boundary was now seven miles south of the Somme, and with the shift, General de Lisle's new divisional front centered on Sailly-Sallisel.

Plans to truck the Newfoundland Regiment as far forward as Guillemont had to be abandoned when a thaw followed by rain made roads impassable. The Regiment ended up having to march more then 25 miles to Bouleaux Wood, where they relieved the Lancashire Fusiliers in the firing line just north of Sailly-Saillisel. They were there three days, during which time they were under heavy enemy shelling. By the time the Regiment withdrew on February 25, four men were dead, nine wounded and three had been gassed.

The Regiment was almost immediately sent back to the front line trenches, where they were temporarily attached to the 86th Brigade, which had been assigned to carry out one of three minor operations assigned by General Rawlinson.

The 86th Brigade's attack began on the last day of February with a heavy artillery bombardment.

After a struggle, the assaulting battalions gained their first objective, Potsdam Trench, about 150 yards east of their own front line, as well as a portion of their final objective, Palz Trench.

The Newfoundland Regiment took over the newly won trenches that night.

A few days later, on March 3, small parties of Germans began bombing inwards from both ends of Palz Trench. Other Germans, concealed by heavy mist and the use of smoke bombs, advanced on each side of the trench and were within about 700 yards before they were discovered.

The Newfoundlanders managed to get an SOS off to headquarters before communication by telephone was cut off and, with all their Lewis guns out of action, resorted to using bombs until more guns could be brought up. The Germans succeeded in getting into the trench and drove the Newfoundlanders out for a distance of 40 yards, to the head of the communications trench. Just when the situation seemed desperate, British guns began a barrage which kept German reinforcements from coming forward.

Seizing the opportunity, Lieutenant Gerald Byrne quickly organized a bombing squad. He grabbed a pail of grenades, led an attack southward along Palz Trench, and succeeded in driving the enemy out.

Byrne and his men followed the Germans into their own territory and drove them out of 50 yards of their front trench.

Lieutenant Byrne was awarded the Military Cross for his initiative in this engagement. Two other men, Private John Lewis and Lance Corporal Martin Picco, were decorated for their bravery in the action.

Lewis received the Military Medal for voluntarily carrying bombs forward during the German barrage. Picco received the Distinguished Conduct Medal because, even though he had been wounded earlier in the day, he continued bombing throughout the whole attack and remained in charge of the advanced position until relieved during the night. By the time they were relieved on March 3, the Regiment had suffered casualties of 27 killed and 44 wounded.

The tiny village of Meaulte, where the Newfoundland Regiment came on March 5, 1917, for a two week stay in billets, was part of a main route to the British Fourth Army's front.

During the months of the Battle of the Somme it is said more than 3,000,000 Allied soldiers marched along Meaulte's main road.

In Meaulte, the Newfoundlanders had an unexpected and very pleasant visit from the Regimental band who arrived from Ayr just in time for St. Patrick's Day.

On the morning of their arrival, the band woke their still sleeping countrymen by playing the rousing "Banks of Newfoundland," which had been arranged as a march and adopted as the official Regimental march.

The band played for daily parades and Sunday church parades and, in what was its most highly acclaimed performance, almost brought the walls of the YMCA hut down when it played on March 17, St. Patrick's Day.

The star of the Paddy's Day concert was Private Esau Penny, when he got up and sang more than 20 verses of his ballad "Number 9" to the tune of Clementine.

Penney, the regimental cook, had first sung this song in Gallipoli and the verses grew as the war progressed. The following is just a sampling:

When the Germans came to Verdun,
Found a train upon the line,
How they swore when they discovered
Forty trucks of Number 9 .
Part of another verse noted,
All the officers get port and brandy,
But the privates, Number 9.
The song always ended:
On my headstone write this line
Esau Penny, First Newfoundland,
Mortally wounded by Number 9. [32]

The year 1916 had been the most bloodstained in history. By the end of the year all those involved in the war has lost so much that no conceivable gains could be adequate compensation. Both sides were now fighting for survival.

On March 14, 1917, there was surprising news that the Germans had begun falling back on a more than 100-mile front extending from the city of Arras to the Aisne River. The withdrawal ended in a new double defence line of great strength which the Germans called Siegfried-Stelling. To the British, it became known as the Hindenburg Line. While the German withdrawal meant giving up a considerable amount of territory, it allowed General Erich Ludendorff to shorten his line by 25 miles and free 13 divisions for deployment elsewhere.

During the latter part of March, the British Fourth and Fifth Armies followed up the German retreat. Field Marshal Haig's plan was to strike a heavy blow at the enemy in Belgium, along a 12-mile front stretching from the city of Lens in the north to Arras in the south. Preparations for the offensive, which would be carried out by the Third and First Army, included a tremendous concentration of artillery, roughly 120,000 men in the storming line and 40,000 in support.

The River Scarpe, flowing eastwards from Arras, split the 12-mile battle front of the two British armies, the great barrier of Vimy Ridge rose to the north. Vimy Ridge ran from the northwest to the southeast between Lens and Arras. The main height of land was four miles long, with its highest point only 475 feet above sea level. It was its command of the valley of the Scarpe River and the Douai Plain that made it an important tactical feature. The ridge was the keystone of the defenses linking the new Hindenburg Line to the main German lines leading north to the Flemish coast, and its capture was seen as essential for success. The Germans had held Vimy Ridge since 1914, and three French attacks in 1914 and 1915 had failed to dislodge them. By 1917, more than 200,000 men had fallen on the long, gentle slopes leading to the crest of the ridge.

The capture of Vimy Ridge, which was the main task of the First Army, was assigned to the Canadian Corps of four divisions. The Third Army's front extended from a point two and a half miles north of the Scarpe to Croiselles, a village eight miles southeast of Arras. The Third Army's objective was to break through enemy defenses, capture the Hindenburg Line and then advance on the village of Cambrai. The goal was to penetrate five miles into enemy territory within the first 12 hours and so open the way for the cavalry.

On a hill five miles from Arras and not far from the Arras-Cambrai road, rising 200 feet above the Scarpe, was the village of Monchy-le-Preux, which up to that time had been virtually untouched by war. Between Arras and Monchy, the Germans held three strongly defended lines of trenches. The Third Army attached great importance to the commanding height of Monchy and made its capture a priority objective.

The first blow of the offensive was to be delivered on April 9, 1917, Easter Monday.

The attack was preceded by intense bombardment of the German's first and second line trenches. At 5:30 a.m. in a driving sleet storm, the infantry launched the first in what turned out to be a seven-week series of struggles which came to known as the Battles of Arras, 1917.

By nightfall on April 9, Canadian troops, commanded by Lieutenant-General Sir Julian Byng, had captured two-thirds of Vimy Ridge. By the end of the second day, the Canadians held all except the northern tip of the ridge.

The Battle of Vimy Ridge resulted in the capture of 4,000 German prisoners, 54 guns, 104 trench mortars and 124 machine guns.

Total Canadian casualties at Vimy Ridge were 10,602, of which 3,598 men died.

Despite heavy Canadian casualties, the Battle of Vimy Ridge was celebrated as a victory. It was, in fact, the greatest victory of the war up to that time.

While the British Third Army, fighting at the Scarpe on the Canadian right, did not achieve all of its first day objectives they had, by the evening of April 9, advanced three and a half miles, a distance not equaled since trench warfare came to the Western Front in 1914.

On April 11, following three days of heavy fighting on the part of both the infantry and the cavalry, Monchy-le-Preux was taken in the face of a devastating bombardment by the enemy. By evening, the village of Monchy was in ruins and its rubble filled centre piled high with the bodies of dead horses. ✹

The Men Who Saved Monchy; Back row (left to right) Corporal A.S. Rose, Sergeant W. Pitcher,
Lieutenant Colonel Forbes Robertson, Lieutenant K.J. Keegan, Sergeant C. Parsons, Sergeant J.R.
Waterfield. Front: Private F. Curran, Corporal J.H. Hillier, Private J. Hounsell. Missing from photo
Private V.M. Parsons. Some of the men had received promotions since Monchy
(courtesy The Fighting Newfoundlander)

 chapter twenty one

On March 28, the Newfoundland Regiment left their billets in Camps-en-Amienois and proceeded, with the 29th Division, to Gouy-en Artois, a small town near the city of Arras. Orders were to relieve the battle weary soldiers at Monchy.

When the Newfoundlanders reached Gouy on the evening of April 10 they were greeted by the sight of a long column of Germans captured by the Canadians on Vimy Ridge the day before.

On April 11, the Newfoundlanders marched to Arras and were given orders to enter the firing line that evening. As darkness fell, the men headed down the Cambrai road toward the sound of guns. After a four-mile march they halted at Les Fosses Farm, less than a mile from Monchy, where Lieutenant-Colonel Forbes Robertson set up his headquarters. Seven hundred yards further along, the Newfoundland Regiment relieved two battalions of the 12th Division along a sunken road leading to Monchy.

At 3 a.m. on April 14, Forbes-Robertson ordered an advance in a direction east of Monchy, on a front of about 500 yards.

The objective was the capture of Infantry Hill, 1,000 yards east of Monchy.

The attack was to be carried out by the 1st Essex Regiment and the Newfoundland Regiment under a creeping barrage.

The attacking troops had not advanced far when they were subjected to a strong German counterattack and heavy enemy shelling. As they continued to advance, enemy machine guns were turned on them. Despite the enemy onslaught, the Newfoundlanders reached part of their objective, suffering heavy losses in the process.

The troops who were supposed to advance to the right and left also had heavy losses and before they could advance far they were held up by an onrush of enemy troops. Counter-attacked on three sides, and with no signs of reinforcements, the men put up a desperate struggle against impossible odds.

The Newfoundland Regiment's D Company, commanded by Captain Herbert Rendell, were almost surrounded by a force of nearly 1,000 Germans but they fought on until they were forced to surrender with the enemy only 50 yards away.

It was the same story with C Company, commanded by Captain Rex Rowsell, where small groups of men fought on until they were either killed or captured.

Farther back, A Company, under Lieutenant J. Bemister, managed to temporarily halt two companies of Germans until an enemy shell knocked out their Lewis gun.

All communication by telephone was cut, but shortly after 10 a.m. a wounded man from the Essex Regiment arrived at battalion headquarters to report that all of his battalion were either killed or captured, and that the Newfoundland Regiment had been wiped out.

Forbes-Robertson immediately sent his signalling officer, Lieutenant Kevin Keegan, to find out the exact situation and bring back a report.

Within 20 minutes, Keegan was back to report that there was not a single unwounded Newfoundlander east of Monchy, and that he had seen Germans advancing less than a quarter of a mile away.

Forbes-Robertson immediately ordered Sergeant-Major White to collect every man he could. His intention was to hold off the German onslaught until reinforcements arrived.

Led by the Colonel, a party of 16 men rushed out, arming themselves with weapons and ammunition from dead or wounded soldiers as they ran toward the village. The small headquarters party, which had been reduced to nine by the time they reached the edge of Monchy, established themselves behind the parapet of a short section of unused trench, and shot every German who advanced towards them.

The men were joined an hour and a half later by Corporal John Hillier of St. John's, who was temporarily knocked out by a bursting shell during the rush forward and crawled in from a shell hole.

For four hours, the ten men held their position, at times opening up a series of bursts of rapid fire to fool the enemy into believing they were a bigger, more powerful force.

The soldiers who became known as the boys who saved Monchy included: Lieutenant-Colonel Forbes-Robertson; Corporal John Hillier, Lieutenant Kevin Keegan, Sergeant Ross Waterfield, Private Fred Curran and Corporal Charles Parsons, all of St. John's; Lance Corporal Walter Pitcher from Old Bonaventure; Private Japheth Hounsell of Wesleyville; Private Albert Rose from Flowers Cove; and Private V. M. Parsons of the Essex Regiment.

Concerning this engagement, Sir Arthur Conan Doyle said:

It was an unsuccessful day, and yet it was one of those failures which will be remembered where facile successes have been forgotten, for it brought with it one episode which elicited in the highest degree the historical qualities of British Infantry.

Regarding the headquarters staff, Father Nangle, in a lecture on the work of the Regiment, said:

Lieutenant-Colonel Forbes-Robertson and his men are the men who saved Monchy. They won fame for themselves; they won fame for the Regiment. The whole British army in France honours the names of these nine men for their heroic conduct.

In fighting on April 14, the Newfoundland Regiment suffered losses only exceeded by those at Beaumont Hamel the previous year.

Between April 12 to 15, a total of 166 men were either killed or died of their wounds; 141 men were wounded and 153 captured, of whom 28 died while in enemy hands.

By the time the fighting ended on April 14 the enemy had succeeded in recovering the ground captured by the Newfoundlanders and the Essex and in cutting those two battalions to pieces. They had not, however, retaken Monchy.

Probably Major General de Lisle, Commander of the 29th Division, was not greatly exaggerating when he told the Newfoundlanders that if Monchy had fallen on April 14 it would have taken 40,000 men to recapture it.

For its part in the battle, the Newfoundland Regiment was awarded the Battle Honour "Arras 1917," which was approved for emblazonment on the Colours.

Before the Newfoundland Regiment left the Arras sector they were involved in another operation, the Second Battle of Scarpe, on April 23.

The Newfoundlanders , who were responsible for guarding the right flank of the 88th Brigade on the Arras-Cambrai road immediately south of Monchy, held their position all day under continual shelling and machine gun fire. Casualties included 13 men killed and 50 wounded.

On May 11, the Regiment returned to Arras for what would be its final tour of duty in the Monchy sector. On May 14, the men took over some old German trenches at Tilloy, a couple of miles east of Arras, next to the Cambrai road. Three days later, the 88th Brigade returned to the line and the Newfoundlanders moved about a mile north of Tilloy to take over dugouts in Railway Triangle, a switching point on the railway, just south of the River Scarpe.

By the end of May, when the Newfoundlanders were relieved by the Essex Regiment, fighting strength was down to 221 men. [33]

For its participation in the Battles of Arras, the Newfoundland Regiment was awarded the Battle Honour "Scarpe, 1917."

Jim Stacey arrived in Monchy on April 12.

Monchy Le Preux

We were in and out of the line until the end of March then moved back to the same village where we had spent Christmas, Champs-en-Amienois, for a few days. About April 9th we were on the march again. As we moved out, we could hear the boom of guns in the distance. We did not know where we were or where we were going - that is the rank and file. We marched all-day and put up for the night at a village and were off again the next morning. The billeting officer went ahead and everything went off like clockwork. The Transport and Cookers followed in the rear. The cooks on the move cooked our skilly. As we carried on each day the sound of guns got nearer. On April 12th just before dark we arrived in the vicinity of Arras. We had marched thirty miles. Leaving our transport behind we carried on to the Arras-Cambrai Road to Feuchy Chapel Corner. Just beyond and to the right we found a well-built house that must have been the German Quartermaster Stores as we found some bully beef there.

We arrived on 12th April, a few days after the Canadians started their Vimy Ridge offensive. On the outskirts of the Arras suburbs ran the jumping off trench. That same night, in darkness, the Companies moved into their positions. Their objective, they were to find out, was Infantry Hill, that was on top of the slope just outside Monchy on the Arras - Cambrai Road. "A" Company was just off the road and Headquarters was in the chalk pit at Les Fosse's farm. The Companies had to dig their jumping off trench that night as they took up their positions. The Company runners were required to report to Battalion Headquarters and bring Headquarters Runners back to their respective Companies. Thus ensuring Headquarters and Companies would know where to find each other. There was an uneasy quietness as they took up their positions.

The next morning about 10:00 a.m., 13 April, Adjunct Raley gave me a message for the CO and said that I would find him at Monchy-le-Preux. I was to take another runner with me, Steve Reid. We went around the high ground and entered Monchy in the rear so we would not be exposed. It was a distance of three-quarters of a mile. Monchy clearly was a sorry sight. It had not been disturbed since being taken four days previously by the Rifle Brigade. There were dead lying everywhere, mostly of the Rifle Brigade and not many of the enemy. We passed through the village and could see no one alive as we searched for Major Forbes-Robertson. We were on the point of giving up the search. Then, as we entered the back yard of a house, we saw what appeared to be a dead man lying on a piece of galvanized corrugated iron. As we passed, he spoke and told us he had been there for four days and wanted to know if we could get him out of there. He took my mind off the search for the CO, which seemed hopeless anyway. I suggested to Reid that we should go back to Battalion Headquarters and get stretcher-bearers to get the man out of the area. When I informed Raley that I had not delivered the message to the CO, he said, "Make haste, get your dinner and go back, you must find him." He asked me if I wanted to take Reid back with me. I told him no as I wanted to get Company stretcher-bearers. Sgt. A. Hammond of the Red Cross and two stretcher-bearers went back with me. The Adjunct said it was vitally important to deliver the message to the CO, so we headed back. The stretcher-bearers evacuated the wounded man. I can safely say he was the last man to be taken out of Monchy, on a stretcher, for the next thirty-six hours.

I was now looking for the CO by myself. After walking around and looking everywhere I saw someone in the distance enter the basement of a house. I followed him slowly. This was an orderly returning to his Battalion Headquarters. He belonged to the 1st. Essex Regiment of our Brigade. Sure enough there was Forbes-Robertson, the man to whom I was to deliver the message. I gave it to him. He read it and then handed it to the CO of the Essex Regiment, who read it and said, "Robertson you should not be here. Your place is back at your Regiment's Headquarters." They looked at one another as if in trouble. Robertson looked at me and asked, "Do you know where "C" and "D" Companies are in the front line?" I said I did not but the other runners knew, as during an advance there were four extra runners taken on. He said that I was to take the message to both Company Commanders and to come with him. He took me down a road facing the firing line. Looking through an opening in the hedge, he pointed to open ground. He said, "C" Company is over there." I looked but I did not see any troops, all I could see was the firing line. I must have been a sitting duck if they wanted to pot me.

Off I went with a message for "C" and "D" Companies. On the left I saw some troops who I thought were "C" Company but they turned out to be an Artillery Observation Post. I asked them if they knew of any troops nearby. They said that there were some, a little further on and to the right. Running in that direction I found "B" Company. Captain B. Butler told me that "C"

Company was on his left, along the side of Infantry Hill just on the outskirts of Monchy. I could see a long distance beyond our line but there was an uneasy stillness. Reaching "C" Company I delivered the message to Captain R.S. Rowsell. As he read the message, I was standing on top of the trench looking down and noticed all the men "standing to" with their bayonets fixed. Rowsell gave a sigh of relief, and said to me, "Those two copses you see are our objective." They were at the bottom of Infantry Hill, Bois du Sart and Bois du Vert, about a quarter of a mile away from where we were standing. "What do you think of it?" he said. I said, "It looks like a hard nut to crack." The only thing Rowsell was waiting for was the artillery support. "I think so too," said he. I moved along to "D" Company and delivered the message. Their position was just on the outskirts of Monchy. Captain Rendell, the Company Commander asked me if I was thirsty and wanted a drink. He might have meant whiskey or rum, but I did not take it that way. I said, "No." I wanted to return to Headquarters as the best of the day had gone. I learned later that a great number were killed and taken prisoner in the ensuing battle. Capt. Rowsell of "C" Company was one of those killed. Rumours were getting around that the Battalion was planning to attack at 5:30 a.m. The Companies stayed in their same positions but Battalion Headquarters had to be moved to Monchy. Most of the Headquarters' staff had moved off before dark. Capt. Kevin Keegan, Bombing Officer, was in charge of Headquarters' details. He came to me and said that I was to be the guide and bring those that remained of the staff. This included the Doctor, Red Cross and Signal Units. There were about a dozen in all. They were leaving at midnight. Keegan placed a map of Monchy on the table. He pointed to a place and said, "That is where our Headquarters is going to be for the advance." I had been in Monchy twice and it was the first time I had seen a map of the village. He pointed out a spot on the map that had to be found in the dark since the Battalion was going over the top at 5:30 a.m. I did not say it was impossible. I knew if I had asked him whether he, an officer could have found it he would have to say no because he had never been to Monchy. I did not tell him that I had been there before. I thought that all I had to do was find Essex Headquarters and get an Essex runner to take us to our headquarters. I was sure they would know so I did not worry.

When the time came our party moved off. It was a very dark morning, with no moon and the stillness was uncanny. We encountered no trouble on our way to the village. There was a German shell dump in the centre of the village and an occasional shell landed into it. There is one thing that still stands out in my memory: A shell had burst just ahead of us on the road. As we passed along, we saw a wounded man rolling on the ground. No one stopped or said a word, but kept straight on going, although we had a Doctor and a Red Cross Unit with us. The rules of the Army were, if you had an objective you could not delay, which could have been be an excuse, on reaching it. We carried on to the Essex Headquarters and asked for directions to the

Newfoundland Headquarters. No one knew where it was and that was a bad state of affairs. Someone had blundered. We started out on our own to see if we could find it but our search was to no avail. Time was running out as we trampled along the cobblestone streets that echoed in the stillness. As dawn was breaking we could hear the footsteps of someone running. We halted him. This was a Company runner, who was returning to the front line after reporting to our Headquarters, so we asked him to take us there. The irony of the situation was that Headquarters was in the same yard as that of the wounded man we had found earlier in the day. Headquarters' staff was now together.

I had just settled down when the attack started. Shells began to fly. Our Headquarters was in a basement with about twenty steps leading up to the yard. There were small long windows at ground level that gave light. These windows soon became blocked with falling brick caused by German shelling. Time went on and there was no word from the outside as Monchy was receiving a furious bombardment. At 9:00 a.m., there was still no word regarding the progress of the attack. Our CO, Maj. Forbes-Robertson, told me to go out and to see if there was anything I could see or find out. I went out on the main road and saw an Essex Sergeant passing. He was wounded in the leg and on his way back. I asked him to come and see our CO. He refused at first but then he followed me into Headquarters. The CO asked him about the advance. He said that the two regiments, Newfoundland and Essex were surrounded. Captain Keegan went out to investigate and his report was not very pleasant. The CO said, "Stand to." Up the stairs he went, grabbing a rifle and a bandoleer from a dead man. The rest followed him. When I reached the yard, a shell burst alongside me and knocked me to the ground. When I came to my senses, I was all right but a little shaken. No one was in sight and I thought it was serious, so I started to look for the rest of Headquarters. Monchy was the key point for the Germans and us. As they kept up the fire, I sought shelter in a cellar. It must have been a German Officer's quarters. There was a fancy table with a cloth. It was all out laid nice and clean. In fact, the table was laid for a meal, which must have been in progress when they were attacked four days earlier. I took stock of this and then my eyes fell on a German with a bandage around his head. He looked at me as if he were alive. His arm was under the table and he could have been holding a bomb. He may have been dead but I was not taking any chances. I quickly got out of there and had passed further on down the street when I heard a tremendous noise above the roar of exploding shells. An exploding small arms ammunition dump caused this noise. A High Explosive shell hit it. I noticed something was burning on the side of the road so I investigated. Here was the body of a member of the Rifle Brigade killed during the attack on the 11th. He had several Very light flares with a flare pistol on his body and the flares had ignited. While searching everywhere to find the rest of the Headquarters' staff, I saw a man, limping around, searching dead bodies. The dead was everywhere and looked as if they had just dozed into a sleep. Most looked so peaceful that I had an urge to wake them. The man was taking the rations and water bottles from the bodies. He used them to help keep six wounded alive. There were five of ours and one German who were in a cellar alongside. They had been there for four days and he was the only one who could get around. He wanted to know if I could get him and the others removed to safety. I told him that I would try. I knew our First Aid Post was close to Essex Headquarters so I told him to follow me. I do not think they got out that day. The ADMS, who were supposed to send up stretcher-bearers, could not get through, so any wounded that could not walk were not evacuated that day.

Just before we reached the brick root cellar that housed our First Aid Post a shell struck it. It immediately collapsed, burying most of the wounded. It was a heart-rending scene as any that saved themselves were covered in brick dust. One of those became to me pointing to his mouth. He could not speak and wanted a drink of water. Art Herder, who was wounded in the arm, was also covered in brick dust. Lt. Jack Bemester asked me how to get back to Monchy. I told him he would have to take his chances because Brigade Headquarters thought Monchy fell to the Germans. Our luck was not with us at Monchy as a whole German Division was poised to attack us that morning. There were several wounded buried alive when the shell struck the First Aid Post, so Art Herder told me in 1954. He was in touch with the War Graves Commission soon after the war. They wanted him to go to France and show them where the First Aid Post had been located. They wanted to place the bodies in a cemetery. He did not go, as they wanted him to pay the expenses. On reaching the First Aid Post, or what remained of it, Dr. J. Tocher who was in charge, told me to stay with him. He wanted me as a guide to take him and the Red Cross Orderlies out when relieved. So I stayed. I was trying to get some sleep while I waited but a wounded casualty was making so much noise that I could not get any rest. I spoke to the Doctor about the noise and he said that it would soon be over. The man was wounded in the back. His lung was punctured and air was wheezing out of the wound.

When we were finally relieved, we went to Arras where we joined ranks and proceeded to a village just outside the town for a few days' rest. After a week we were back in supports again. The 86th and 87th Brigades were in the line on the right of Monchy facing Guemappe. I was in a house on the Arras-Cambrai Road that was on high ground. From the window, I had a full view of the ridge in front of Guemappe. I could clearly see the plain that ran to my right and to the rear. I saw a wave or line of troops right across the plain coming up from the rear. At first it seemed foolish for troops to be exposing themselves, as they would draw fire. As I watched I saw another wave a fair distance behind the first and so on. It dawned on me when they reached the ridge that this must be an attack. The shells started to come over and the troops came on. Then the machine gun bullets started to fly. I peeked over the sandstone windowsill until it became too hot for my presence. By now bullets began to hit the side of the house. I clearly had a bird's eye view of the whole advance.

They failed in their attempt to take their objective.

The next day Battalion Headquarters was in a trench at Orange Hill. The Regiment again went into the line about a half mile in front of Les Fosses Farm, their objective being Machine Gun Wood. Other Battalions of the 88th Brigade were also in the attack. Orange Hill, at the bottom of the high ground, was about halfway between the front line and the Feuchy Road. From our trench we had a good view of the road when the attack started. The battery of 25 pounders advanced just past our support trench and unlimbered to support the advance. I do not think they were of much help because the enemy put down a barrage and the gunners had to leave their guns unmanned. The 9.2's were down Euchy Road. We were in the middle, which was the safest place, watching the German shellfire. You would think that the German fire had blown up the gun as it disappeared in the smoke. This was the first time I saw a wireless operator with earphones on, manipulating dials on a radio set as he contacted the planes overhead. The battle progressed later into the day and the front line was running short of small arms ammunition, so about a dozen men were detailed to take some there. Each had two bandoleers, 100 rounds, slung over their shoulders and they had to make it in the face of heavy fire. I do not know how many made it or came back. Power, who did not make it back, was under age. He had his pass in his pocket to return to the 2nd Battalion Headquarters in England, to stay until he was old enough to enlist.

As a Battalion Runner, I had to take messages to Brigade Headquarters, which generally was a good distance from our Battalion. On a particular trip, I had to pass through the outskirts of Arras. This was where the old front line ran, which had not moved since the start of the war. Here, behind the former German line, I had a chance to see their strong points such as the Harp and Triangle. You could see some of what the Canadians had to overcome. Every house and even the streets had disappeared. I noticed several civilians with two local policemen and they all seemed excited. They were digging up the ground and searching around a back yard of what was the foundation of a house a trench passed close by. An elderly man pointed to a spot and said, "Ici." It was close to the trench. They dug and unearthed a box that contained the family treasures that they had buried in their back yard in 1914, to keep them from the invading Germans.

I had to avoid the main Arras-Cambrai road, which was a straight road lined with trees between towns. For safety reasons, I never used the road because the trees were a mark for the gunners. I would always give myself at least a two-hundred-yard space from the road because I never knew when a salvo would strike. The Battalion was at low ebb - 49 killed, 142 wounded and 296 missing after the Monchy battle.

Rest and Relaxation

For a rest, the Regiment went to Berneville about three miles from Arras. It was here that the BBC, with their cameras, took a film of the whole Battalion marching past and we even posed for stills. Meanwhile, we did receive reinforcements. Lt. Col. Hadow returned to Berneville after four months on leave. The first thing he said when he saw me was, "Hello Stacey, you still here?" A move was made right away to send all old vets, wounded or otherwise, for a rest. This included all those who had not been away from the Battalion for the last six months and this included, for endurance, the worst six months of the war. There were about twenty in all, with Captain Keegan in charge. We went to the 5th Army Rest camp on the beach at Equires, about twelve kilometres from Boulonge. We were in for a good holiday with just rest and army rations. The pay we received was fifteen francs, that was five francs or one dollar a week. A few of the boys including myself had a chance to go to Boulonge in a Red Cross ambulance to see the sights. In all our travels the large towns were always out of bounds for the other ranks.

In Boulonge I noticed a bank, Coxes Bank of London, in which the army WACS were the clerks. A thought struck me to try to cash a cheque on the Bank of Montreal. Thinking that fifteen francs pay would not go far, and there was no harm in trying, I wrote out a cheque for two hundred and fifty francs. I wrote in No. 466, Cpl. A.J. Stacey, Royal Newfoundland Regiment, and B.E.F. France. I passed it to the clerk who asked no questions, but passed me the two hundred and fifty francs. You can be sure that I was the happiest boy. The rest had only fifteen francs and the Sergeants had twenty-five.

The 5th Army Rest Camp was very large. I think every Regiment of the British Army came to rest here. I met two friends with whom I went to school at Benson, Oxford, England. In 1961 while visiting England, I met Len Snuggs who mentioned the camp to me. It had a lovely beach with fine sand and it was a fine place to swim. There were all kinds of sports with competitions and prizes were given to the winners. I won first prize for a pillow fight on poles. It was exciting. We all lined up for our prizes that were in an envelope. I never did have a chance to see the contents as everyone was giving his envelope to the Red Cross and of course I could be no different.

After our allotted time we returned fully refreshed and ready to carry on. As the summer approached, the days became hotter. To accommodate the heat the rules on route marches were changed. We would fall in at dawn, do our route marches and be off duty before the heat of the day.

On the next day's orders the whole Battalion, including all details such as Officers servants, cooks, and Battalion runners, would go on a route march. In fact, all except the Battalion police were to go. They would be left behind to look after all the billets. We were to fall in at 3 a.m. I am sorry to say that the three runners and I overslept. The Officer's mess cook, the CO's orderly, the adjunct's orderly and a few more of headquarters' staff were in the same boat. We disobeyed an order and by doing so we had to go before the orderly room CO. For such a crime we would get pay stopped. What Captain Keegan, who was in charge of Headquarters staff, and I could not understand was, why we *were not up for this crime with the others. That is another mystery of the war.*

Letters and Parcels

There was a Lance Corporal detailed to look after the Battalion mail. He had to take the outgoing mail to the Brigade's post office and pick up the incoming mail. Also each day the Division mail truck delivered Division's incoming mail to Brigade Headquarters and picked up their outgoing for the return trip. Because of the overlap, every day, our mailman had a long wait for the incoming mail as it had to be sorted. Then he had to make the long journey back to Battalion. If it were only letters or only one bag it could be managed on the bicycle. Otherwise a transport had to be used to deliver it. When the Battalion was in the line, the mailman sent letters and papers, up with the rations, to the respective Companies. Parcels and registered letters were held back until the recipient came out of the line and personally picked them up. When we moved to Berneville, the Post Orderly put all of the mail, including the parcels and registered letters, into a limber. On arrival at their destination the registered letters were missing, so he said, but Hadow did not think so. All registered letters and parcels had to be signed for, all the way through and kept track of in a logbook. When the recipient received his registered letter or parcel he had to sign the log for it. In this instance, the registered letters were lost so he crossed them out of the book. That was all right for the time being. When an owner inquired about a registered letter, it was traced from the fountainhead to the Regiment. The CO asked to see the book and saw all the missing letters crossed out. The upshot was the Lance Corporal received ninety days field punishment. I was then placed in charge of the mail and given a lecture on how important it was. Bert Dicks was placed in charge of me.

All letters had to be censored. The procedure to follow, after you wrote your letter, was to put it in an unsealed envelope and then give it to your Company Officer. He would read it to see if there was anything of military importance that should not be told. If there were, it would be sent to the orderly room where it was rubber stamped with "Censor," parts were blacked out and a number marked on it. The letter would be returned to you so that you could rewrite it. If it were all right the envelope would be franked. All the letters were then placed in a sandbag and away you went on your bike to Brigade Post Office. This was generally with the Army Service Corps, and might be two or three miles away. On reaching the Battalion Post Office of the 88th Brigade, you would turn in the mail that you had and pick up any that was addressed to your Regiment. In this location there were two postmen from London, who were sent to look after the Brigade's mail. There were four post orderlies beside myself and on occasion we had to wait for the 29th Division mail truck to arrive. If we had any money, we would go to a nearby cafe to quench our thirst. If the mail was mostly letters, all we had to do was put them into a bag and away we would go for home. If there were parcels we had to return with the Officer's mess covered-in cart and sometimes it took up the whole day. When the Brigade was on the move the Brigade Post Office would tell me the day before where I could find them to pick up their mail. Putting my belongings and surplus mail aboard a limber belonging to transport, I would jump on the bike and away I would go on my own.

I had a letter of mine censored and I might add it was the last time. The Officer who censored my letter was Captain Frost. Afterwards I procured what was known as "green envelopes." You could seal them but had to sign your name to the effect that there was no military information contained therein. There would be a box of "green envelopes" come through the mail once a month. The orderly room would distribute so many to the Orderly Sergeant for the Companies. You could be sure that Headquarters' staff had their share- we always had a few on hand. They were just as valuable as money. If we wanted something to eat like a tin of pork and beans or a loaf of bread, all we had to do was to go to the Army Service Corps that handled the Division's rations and use a green envelope to pay for it. It would not only get you one tin of beans but two if you wanted them.

We also had a post card called the "whiz bang." It was printed for you and all you had to do was to cross out the sentences or words which did not apply to your case such as:

I am in hospital (or leaving).
I am feeling fine (or sick).
I am leaving hospital for home (or line).
Will be seeing you in a short time.
Will be going home on leave shortly.
Hope to see you soon.

They were very convenient for people in hospital who could not write letters to let their parents know that they were all right. The parcels that arrived for those killed in action or considered missing given to the Orderly Sergeant to be distributed to the men of their Company. No sender wished the return of their parcels.

I pitied the rank and file as they had to be in full marching order. In most cases I would go a different way in order to pass through a town if possible so I could buy a decent meal. No one worried about you as long as the mail arrived. As I said before, when I took over the mail I was given a lecture on how important the mail was and how I should look after it. I started out in good faith. Two days later we were on the move. On arriving at the Battalion's new quarters the billeting officer had a billet for me with no door. I thought it was not a safe place for mail, especially parcels, in my absence. I went to the CO and asked what should be done in my absence as the responsibility rested with me. His advice was to tie up the bags with parcels in them and seal them with wax. I considered that but it was just as easy to lose a bag as a parcel.

Another time I complained to Captain Bert Dicks, and he asked me if I wanted a chateau. I gave up complaining after that and did my best. The registered letters were my biggest headache, as they had to be kept on my person at all times and under my head when sleeping. I had them in a German knapsack that was just large enough for letters only. The knapsack was smaller than ours was and more suitable to put under your head at night while sleeping.

Another problem was registered parcels. I had one for Corporal Hann who happened to be on a machine gun course and would not be back for another week. I could not carry it with me so I had to leave it in my billet when I went each day for the mail. The parcel for Cpl. Hann was from the United States. His sister had registered the parcel to make sure he would get it. To make a long story short, the parcel disappeared. I was in a sweat now wondering whether to report it right away or not. I did not have much success reporting before, so I decided to wait until Hann came back and explain the whole thing to him. My impression was that the parcel contained a few smokes and candy. The day before Hann was due to return another parcel arrived for him. When he finally returned, I delivered the second parcel and explained about the first that was stolen. He did me a good turn by signing for both in the registration book.

I always had a considerable amount of mail and parcels on hand. Drafts for reinforcements would go first to Rouen, and often the mail would arrive before the owner. There was also mail for hospitals sent to the wrong clearing stations. You would get their address from the orderly room and send the mail on. Before they would get it they would probably be moved to the Battalion or back to England. It was no easy job. People in Newfoundland began to complain that their parcels were not received overseas. The Pay and Records office in London had a bright idea that every parcel sent overseas, would definitely reach the owner according to the system they would set up. All Newfoundland mail went to the Pay and Records Office at Victoria Street, London, first. There it would be re-addressed and sent to each Regiment, 1st Battalion in France, 2nd Battalion in Scotland or afterwards England. Each parcel had a consignment number such as 1/1, 1/2, 1/3 and so on. Included in the mailbags were triplicate forms, which had the registration number and name of the Owner. All I had to do, as Mail Clerk, was to get the signature of the Owner or that of the Orderly Sergeant who would deliver it to the owner's Company. Most of the people at Pay and Records Office forgot that there was a war on and that conditions were not what they were used to. When the mail arrived, I would have to deliver the parcels and obtain the signatures by myself. Some of the parcels went missing, therefore, there were some blanks on the forms. I was told afterwards that the parcels were stolen from behind my back. The forms had to be returned to Pay and Records Office. What could I do? If the forms went back with blanks, how could I explain? I could say they were destroyed by enemy action but instead I took the path of least resistance. I filled in the blanks myself but not with my own name, of course. I knew it was wrong and I could have gone to the CO or Bert Dicks but from past experience that would be of no use. I never ever heard any complaints about it. ✸

▓ *chapter twenty two*

In Britain, during the summer of 1917, several institutions in London came up with the idea of making the 420th anniversary of John Cabot's discovery of Newfoundland an occasion to pay tribute to the heroism of Newfoundland's soldiers.

The project was well covered by the London press. An editorial in the Times posed the question: "Why should London be asked to observe Newfoundland Week?" and then proceeded to answer its own question. *"Newfoundland is our oldest colony. It is outside the usual lines of world traffic and until recent years few strangers called there. Its total population is far less than Camberwell and only a little more than St. Pancras- fishermen, lumbermen, planters.*

Can a small, remote and comparatively poor community like this act in a way that will stimulate the whole spirit of the Empire? The deeds of the Newfoundlanders show that it is." [34]

Six organizations joined in sponsoring Newfoundland Week: the Royal Colonial Institute, the British Empire League, the Victoria League, the British Empire Club, the Overseas Club and the Newfoundland War

Contingent Association.

The organizations had trouble finding Newfoundland soldiers to participate as the 1st Battalion was fighting in Flanders, the 2nd Reserve Battalion was training in Scotland, and the only Newfoundland soldiers in London were those recovering in military hospitals such as Wandsworth.

Fortunately, the Regimental Band was available and arrangements were made for it to visit London. The band had a full week with at least two concerts a day. Wherever the band went in London it was accompanied by the regimental mascot, the Newfoundland dog named Sable Chief, led by Private Hazen Fraser.

Meanwhile, back at the Western Front, the long-planned French offensive at the Aisne, to which the early Arras battles were a prelude, was launched on April 16 and proved a tragic failure.

This, coupled with the inconclusive termination of the Battles of Arras meant the Allies had to develop a new strategy.

At a joint French-British military conference in Paris on May 4, it was decided that the original plan of a massive breakthrough in 1917 would have to be abandoned.

Allied attacks would, instead, be confined to attacks with limited objectives, with the aim of wearing down the enemy and preventing the launch of a counter attack.

The campaign intended to bring victory on the Western Front was postponed until 1918, by which time it was expected American troops would have arrived in France in considerable numbers.

Haig now turned to a long thought about offensive through Flanders, with the object of securing the Belgian coast and reaching the Dutch border.

In its initial phase, the British offensive succeeded brilliantly.

On June 7, 1917, the British took the strategically important village of Messines, the heights of which commanded miles of German occupied territory. Within a week, the front line from Armentieres to the Menin Road was straightened, thus ending German domination of the Ypres Salient from the south.

When the 29th Division transferred to the 5th Army at the end of June and took up position three miles north of Ypres, the Newfoundland Regiment was assigned duties which included occupying the firing trenches, repairing trenches and bringing up supplies under enemy shelling.

Between July 6 and July 12, ten Newfoundlanders were killed and 23 wounded.

The Third Battle of Ypres, also known as the Passchendaele Campaign, began on July 31 and didn't end until November 10 when Canadian infantrymen captured the village of Passchendaele.

Canadian casualties over this period numbered 15,654.

The Battle of Langemarck began at dawn on August 16, starting off at the Steenbeek River, when the Newfoundland Regiment's Companies B and C, closely followed by Company A and D, crossed the Steenbeek and began moving towards three successive objectives, the Blue Line, the Green Line and the Red Line, spaced approximately 500 yards apart.

Advancing over mud and swamp behind a creeping barrage, the Newfoundland Regiment reached their objectives, enabling the 4th Worcesters and the 1st Essex to sweep through to their objective, the Broembeek River.

When the Newfoundland Regiment was relieved by troops of the 86th Brigade on the morning of August 17, they moved back behind the Yser Canal to spend a short period in a camp near Elverdinghe.

In the seven weeks following the Battle of Langemarck, the Regiment shuttled from one camp to another in the rear area around Elverdinghe and Proven. The longest and most recuperative stay was three weeks at Penton Camp, just outside Proven Woods in Flanders.

For the Newfoundland Regiment and the 29th Division, the Battle of Poelcapelle was their last fight in the Passchendaele Campaign. The Newfoundlanders were at Cardoen Camp, not far from Elverdinghe, when orders came regarding the attack.

As in the Steenbeek battle, the advance would be made to three successive objectives.

On the evening of October 7, the Regiment marched through pouring rain to Canal Bank, on the west bank of the Yser, where they spent the night in dugouts.

The following day, they had a march of five hours to reach the front line.

Zero hour was 5:20 a.m.

The plan was that the 4th Worcesters were to carry the attack to the second objective, with the Newfoundland Regiment following and sweeping past to the final objective.

However, in crossing the Broembeek river, the assaulting parties become badly mixed. The result was that some of the Newfoundlanders, who were not supposed to go into battle until the second objective had been captured, found themselves engaged too early.

By noon, however, the Newfoundlanders had reached their objective and consolidated their gains, which covered a front of about 450 yards. [35]

On October 11, the 29th Division, which had suffered 4,700 casualties in the past two months, 1,100 of those since the morning of October 9, were relieved by the 17th Division and began a period of nearly six weeks out of the line.

Newfoundland casualties for the period were 67 killed and 127 wounded.

Among those killed was Transport Officer Lieutenant Stan Goodyear, who died instantly on October 9 when he was struck by a shell while bringing up supplies. Before the end of the year the Grand Falls native was posthumously awarded a Military Cross.

By the time the third Battle of Ypres ended on November 10, 1917, Allied troops had pushed the German lines back five miles, at a cost of 400,000 Allied casualties.

Back to Belgium

The Battalion next moved to Proven Woods in Flanders, which is to the northwest of Poperinge, and was billeted in tents about fifteen miles from the front line. In this sector we were in reserves and supports for four months and where we first experienced being bombed. The Germans were after the ammunition dump so we had sandbags built around each tent. They sent a large Gotha plane, which only came out on moonlight nights to do the bombing. The plane must have been large, by World War I standards, because of the awful noise it made. Our searchlights would try to pick it up in the beams and when they did, the plane would twist out of it. It would be droning around for some time before dropping bombs. They amounted to about a dozen at a time, one after the other. You would hear them whistling through the air and exploding in a line towards our tents. They would certainly give you a scare because you never knew where the next one was going to land.

Another time there was quite a commotion of machine-gun fire. Our own Lewis guns, mounted on poles, were firing at a German plane. There was also the time when a German plane was chased by our fighters. I saw it skimming over the trees losing height. It came down in the woods not far from camp so I ran in that direction. There were two Airmen and one was wounded who, when I arrived, was being bandaged up. This reminded me of a time back on the Somme near Gueudecourt when a German fighter came down just beyond our dugout and trench. The flier was dead but his spotless brown leather gaiters came in very handy to one of our staff as such things were a luxury.

When in Belgium in 1916, our Transport built the transport lines at a place called Vlamertinghe. It was situated half way between Poperinghe and Ypres. On our return in 1917, Brigade Headquarters and the Post Office were using these lines. This was the only time that we were together with Transport and Quartermaster stores. On previous occasions we were at least two miles from Brigade Post Office. There was a chap here who we called Bert, a Mons Vet, and I'll relate to you a story about him. He was one of the two people who handled the Brigade's mail and he was always asking me for a drink of SRD rum. I never could oblige him. The quartermaster's stores controlled all rations, including rum. He would say, in front of all those waiting for their mail, "Newfie, what about that drink you promised me?" Now that we were all in the same area I thought that it was a good chance to fulfill my promise so I asked Quartermaster McNeil if it would be all right to have a friend over for the evening. He said it would. I informed Bert and brought him over to the Quartermaster's stores and introduced him to those present. The refreshment was a half-gallon jar of SRD rum; a pint enamel jug was filled and passed around. It was filled a second time because there were several in the party. When the jug was passed to me I was careful and would only take a sip. The party was now getting happy when the host said, "what about a night cap?" That was another pint, then the guests dispersed. I had to see Bert home. As the ground was low and flat, ditches were provided to drain it and duck-boards were laid across these ditches. As Bert was a little under the weather, I had my hands full getting him over those duck boards without falling into the ditch. The next morning while delivering the mail, I saw Bert at his post looking a little seedy. When I took him to his bunk, which was made of wire netting, the previous night, he must have scratched his face just above his right eye. The blood had run down his face and dried; it did not improve his appearance. He did not say a word to anyone in spite of the others' jokes. I stayed until the others had gone and then he said to me, "I thought I was the master of liquor but not so. No more for me, I'm finished with it." He never asked me for a drink again.

In this sector there was a noticeable crossroads, just like the one at Ginchy on the Somme. It was known as "International Corner" and it was in use continually to bring supplies up the line at night. The German gunners had it marked and no one liked to pass that way.

Poperinghe was a nice sized town about twelve miles from the line. It had been shelled, but not as much as some other places, and while we were there most of the population were gone; a few shopkeepers and cafe owners were still in business. There was one restaurant where you could get a good meal, according to war standards, which I patronized whenever the chance came my way. There was also a branch of a Belgian bank, which provided me with a cheque cashing capability. In order to cash a cheque, one had to get the town Mayor to endorse it. The town Mayor was an English Officer who was a go between for the Army and the Civilians and he had the power to settle all claims. Talbert House, a meeting place for soldiers during the war, also was located in this town.

I once visited the city of Ypres. It must have been a beautiful place according to what I saw of the ruins. Only the shell of the Cloth Hall building and the Cathedral remained. The city had received considerable shellfire. In my wanderings I came across a tower which I climbed to the top of, even though some of the stone steps were knocked out. It was a wonderful view and I had to use my imagination to visualize what the place was like before the war. Ypres took the full brunt of the war right from the beginning. It was considered an anchor town, never taken by the enemy.

That accounts for the fact that the salient was very vulnerable to a gas attack; the wind could blow the gas over on three sides. The Germans used gas when we were there in 1916 but luck was on our side. We were in supports, in Ypres at the time, so it did not reach us although we were prepared. The Hants Regiment who was in the line at the time received the full force of it. The only casualties I saw from that attack were dead rats. In this area also, there was "Hell Fire Corner" that everyone knew about. The name was enough. There also was a place called "Y" Wood that Raley and I could never forget. Other towns situated to the northwest were St. Julien and Elverdinghe. The latter was home to our Battalion Headquarters while we were in reserves.

With all the seriousness of war we had an occasional light side when we were back in supports and reserves. We had to have refreshments that not only refreshed us but gave us a feeling that there was no war on. To obtain these refreshments we sometimes had to go to considerable trouble and we did not mind if we wanted a bottle of whiskey. Whiskey was not for NCO's or other ranks but only for officers. If we at Headquarters wanted a bottle, we had to get an officer to write his signature on a slip of paper stating that he wanted a bottle of whiskey. In one case I took this to the Town Mayor who had to countersign it. The canteen was the only place that you could get whiskey, but the demand was greater than the supply as there were too many, like us, doing the same thing. The Mayor's office closed at 5:00 p.m. I arrived at 5:00 p.m. on the dot. The Mayor was a surly man and barked, "get out of here, it's after five." As I was making for the door he said, "Where are you from?" I said, "Headquarters." His face changed and it seemed that he could not do enough for me. He signed the slip with a smile. I wondered why there was such a change in him. I found out afterward that Col. Hadow had sent his orderly to get a bottle the day before and found all the stocks were depleted at the canteen so he went over to the Mayor to find out the reason. The change came because I was from Battalion Headquarters and he probably thought that I was getting a bottle for the CO.

In our get-together with light refreshments we used to play cards and have a good hearty singsong. I remember to this day, the songs that each sang. QMS Colin Mews would sing, "When I Came From Dixie", Lionel Munn would sing, "Oh You Beautiful Doll", Fred LeGrow would recite, "Gunga Din" by Rudyard Kipling and so on. I remember at the close of the party we would sing in chorus, "La Marseillaise" in German. I don't remember whether or not we sang "God Save the King".

During the month of August the Battalion went into the line in an area that was part of what is known as Flanders Field. On August 15th, at the Steenbeek River, the Battalion advanced over what you would call a floating swamp and gained its objective without too many losses: nine killed, 93 wounded and one missing. What happened in this sector was the same as any other. The mail for the respective Companies, when taken in the front line, was put into sandbags and given to each Quartermaster Sergeant so that it would go up with the rations. I noticed, one particular time after they had gone that the Battalion Headquarters' and the CO's mail was left behind. It would not *be nice for me if Hadow did not get his mail, or his daily newspaper that was included in the Headquarters mail, when the Companies did. So that no one would be disappointed, I jumped on a bicycle in daylight, took the mail and delivered it right up to the front line to Headquarters. A storm of protest was raised. I was told to get under cover to prevent drawing enemy fire. I could see it was not a very healthy place to be with German planes flying low. I made a hasty getaway. Later, after the war, I was working in my store when Jack Long, who had been a Captain at the time, came in with some friends. He pointed his finger at me and said in a loud voice so other customers could hear, "there he is, the one who rode up to the front line on a bicycle." I was told afterward that the place, Wijdendrift Dump, was a very hot spot and especially so after dark.*

After the Steenbeek push we moved back behind the lines for two months. Then on October 8th the Battalion went over the top at Broembeek about three hundred yards south of the Broembeek River. It was not so easy as the Steenbeek stunt. We had 50 killed, 130 wounded and 14 missing. Lt. Stanley Goodyear, Transport Officer, was among those killed. When he was taking up rations, a shell struck the transport killing him and several others.

When I visited Col. Hadow in 1961, Goodyear's name came up and Hadow said he was one of the best officers he had. As Transport Officer, he always delivered the rations to the troops. Hadow went on to tell me that he first met him at Suez. When they moved to Egypt, Col. De Burton, who was our Commanding Officer, retired, and Hadow who was Brigade Major at the time took over as CO of the Newfoundland Regiment. The Transport was not used in Gallipoli and after that campaign the Battalion went to Suez. Hadow went to the Newfoundland Transport lines. There, he said he met a Sergeant and asked him if he knew who he was. "A bloody officer I suppose," said Goodyear.

Lt. Stan Goodyear was killed at what they call "Hellfire Corner".

The same shell that killed Goodyear also killed Quartermaster Sergeant Ned Nichol of "D" Company. Nichol's death developed into quite an episode. I had a registered letter for Private Jones who was up the line in "D" Company. The Orderly Sergeant at the time, Jim Taylor, took "D" Company's mail along with the registered letters and signed for them in my register book. Some time later I was called into the orderly room where the CO asked to see my register book. He took it and asked why a registered letter addressed to Private Jones was found among the personal effects of Nichols and signed for in the register book by Jim Taylor. This took me by surprise, but after a while it dawned on me what exactly happened. All personal effects found on a dead person go to General Headquarters. Jim Taylor gave the letter to Nichol who went up with the rations and was subsequently killed with the same shell that killed Goodyear. ✵

chapter twenty three

On November 17, 1917, the Newfoundland Regiment left billets in the quiet little village of Berles-au-Bois, ten miles from the city of Arras, and marched eight miles to Boisleux au Mont where they boarded trains to Peronne. Seven hours later, they arrived in Peronne where they embarked on a night march to Moislains.

The following day, dusk was falling when they broke camp and began moving forward again, this time to Sorel-le-Grand, a village about five miles away, not far from their former battlefield in Sailly-Saillisel.

A huge concentration of troops had been assembled at Sorel in preparation for a major operation set to be launched on November 20.

Briefly, the aim of the offensive was to capture the city of Cambrai, the commanding height of Bourlon Wood on the left, and the crossings of the Sensee River north of Cambrai.

New tactics, including the use of massed tanks to protect the advancing infantry, were to be used. When the planned breakthrough had occurred, five divisions of the Cavalry Corps would pass through to exploit it.

Haig had assigned the Third Army 19 infantry divisions and 278 fighting tanks, as well as 98 additional tanks to be used for carrying supplies, dragging wire away from the cavalry routes and providing wireless and telephone communications.

On November 19, the troops at Sorel were confined to quarters.

All was quiet as officers carried out a final inspection of equipment and rifles.

The Hindenburg Line, the objective of the next day's battle, was just six miles away.

Proposals for an attack on the Hindenburg Line in front of Cambrai had been made in April, 1917, but the project was put on hold during the prolonged offensive in Flanders. In mid-October, Field Marshal Haig finally gave approval for the Third Army to undertake the operation.

The battle against the Hindenburg Line at Cambrai commenced in the early hours of November 20. Not long after midnight, the troops at Sorel fell in, company by company.

The signal to move out was given at 2:30 a.m.

The Newfoundland Regiment moved off, 17 officers and 536 other ranks. All of the men were heavily laden, each one carrying about 72 pounds, which included 170 rounds of small arms ammunition, a flare and two Mills bombs. A good many carried either a pick or a shovel. The marching troops were led by more than 100 camouflaged tanks and preceded by a surprise artillery attack.

As the troops pressed forward to their objectives, the concentration of men and equipment was so heavy that at one time the Newfoundland Regiment was halted for two hours in a ravine about a mile behind the front.

At about 10 a.m. with everyone at last in position, the more than 12,000 men of the 29th Division moved forward simultaneously. The 88th Brigade placed its four battalions in a diamond formation. At the point, acting as an advanced guard, was the Essex Regiment, with the Newfoundland Regiment and the Worcesters on the left and right flanks, and the Hampshire bringing up the rear.

Following the same formation within the Newfoundland Regiment, Colonel Hadow placed A Company, commanded by Captain Bob Stick at the point of the diamond; D Company under Captain Herbert Rendell was on the left; B Company under Captain Bert Butler was on the right and C Company, under Captain Grant Peterson, was in the rear. [36]

The four tanks leading the advance of the 88th Brigade were put out of action by an enemy field battery which was captured with 150 prisoners in an attack assisted by the Newfoundland Regiment.

When the troops were well into the Hindenburg Support Line, the Newfoundlanders were kept busy clearing numerous German occupied dugouts.

When at last they were out in the open, the men found themselves looking down a slope to the St. Quentin Canal, about 1,000 yards away. To the left was the village of Marcoing. To the right was Masnieres, with the church spires of Cambrai looming in the distance. Half a mile ahead there was a small wood, Marcoing Copse, from which the Newfoundland Regiment was to launch its assault on the St. Quentin Canal.

After reaching the woods, the Regiment was held by heavy enemy machine gun fire which was being directed at their objective, a lock and footbridge west of Masnieres. When a tank unexpectedly appeared and began firing at the Germans, the men took advantage of the diversion and immediately attacked over the bridge. For his part in the capture of the bridge, Captain Grant Peterson was presented with a Bar to his Military Cross.

Next day, the 29th and 20th Divisions received orders to attack east of Masnieres as far as Crevecour. The Newfoundland Regiment was ordered to move to a beet sugar factory on the east side of Masnieres, where it would form the brigade reserve.

As the Newfoundlanders marched along the canal road a shell crashed into their column, killing 10 men and wounding 15 more.

One of those killed was Lance Corporal John Shiwak of Labrador, the Regiment's leading sniper and only Inuit member.

During the first two days of the Battle of Cambrai, the Newfoundland Regiment suffered 54 men killed and 195 men wounded.

On November 22, the Regiment marched through the streets of Masnieres and out to the lock they had won two days earlier. Crossing the footbridge, they continued on past Marcoing Copse to Marcoing. Here, they found rough quarters in the cellars of houses partially demolished by shell fire, and enjoyed hot food supplied by regimental cooks for the first time in several days.

On November 23, the quiet in Marcoing was shattered by enemy field guns, and from then on both Marcoing and Masnieres were under continual shelling.

For four days, the Newfoundlanders occupied trenches on the north side of the canal, returning to the Marcoing cellars at the end of the day.

On November 29, seventy-nine reinforcements arrived. The men were under the command of Captain Rupert Bartlett, who was killed the following day.

On the evening of November 29, the Newfoundland Regiment received orders to carry out a relief in front of Masinieres.

At dawn the next morning, the Germans began heavily shelling the town. By 7 a.m. the whole of Marcoing was enveloped in dense, black smoke. Word soon came that two battalions of the 86th Brigade and the neighbouring Brigade of the 20th Division were facing a strong enemy attack from Crevecoeur south and east of Masinieres.

The Newfoundland Regiment, enroute to take up positions in

Marcoing Copse, were met by advancing German troops attempting to encircle the 29th Division's bridgehead.

Without hesitation, the Newfoundlanders attacked with lowered bayonets and managed to halt the German advance. The Newfoundlanders were soon joined on their right flank by the other battalions of the 88th Brigade, the Essex, the Hampshires, and the Worcesters.

By nightfall, the four battalions had forced the enemy back almost a mile.

As darkness fell, they dug in along a 5000-yard front and held on there for the next 24 hours.

On December 3, the Germans renewed their counterattack and the British soldiers were subject to heavy shell and mortar fire and infantry attacks. The day's battle resulted in 71 casualties for the Newfoundland Regiment.

All told, the grim battle which failed to capture Cambrai represented a British advance of two miles on a five mile front. For the Germans, it resulted in an advance of some four miles.

British losses in the battle numbered more than 40,000. German losses were as much as 5,000 more. [37]

A military report to the British House of Commons later blamed the unsatisfactory results of the Battle of Cambrai on a lack of training of junior officers, non-commissioned officers and men, as well as poor visibility, the enemy's surprise attack and the lack of liaison between the British formations.

There was, however, no criticism of the performance of the Newfoundland Regiment and other units of the 29th Division who had so gallantly defended Masinieres.

Two weeks after the battle, King George awarded the granting of the title "Royal" to the Newfoundland Regiment in recognition of its performance at Cambrai and Ypres.

No other regiment was to have such a distinction awarded during World War I.

Seven years after the First World War had ended, Field Marshal Haig came to St. John's to unveil Newfoundland's National War Memorial. At the ceremony, he chose to talk of the Battle of Cambrai to illustrate the "high courage and unfailing resolution" of the Newfoundlanders who had fought under his command.

For its part in the battle, the Newfoundland Regiment was awarded the Battle Honour "Cambrai 1917" for emblazonment on the Colours.

Sorel and Marcoing

About mid-October we left Belgium and moved behind Cambrai, where there was something secret going on and a little more secret than usual. When we moved, it was at night and during daylight we were under a cover of wire netting laced with artificial green grass. We were given strict orders to keep under cover. The Hindenburg line was especially built to resist frontal attack and was supposed to be impregnable, with barbed wire, and as I was to observe later, it measured several feet thick. An exact duplicate of the line was mapped out behind our front line and the troops practiced taking it in maneuvers. Shortly afterward we moved up to Sorel-Le-Grand leaving there at about 2:30 a.m. on November 20th for the assembly line. The Newfoundland Battalion formed the centre of the 88th Brigade. The Worcesters were on the left and the Essex on the right, with four hundred tanks, which ploughed through the barbed wire and trench system of the Hindenburg line. We took the Germans by surprise passing Marcoing and carrying on into Masnieres which was about six miles from the jumping off place. Sgt. Eaton and I, from the Transport lines at Sorel-Le-Grand, went with the others when Battalion Headquarters was moved to Marcoing on November 30th. Headquarters was situated in a crypt under a church, in the centre of town. Private George Kane and Neil McLellan who had just come back off leave from England went up the line with us. Kane was killed and McLellan was taken prisoner. It was here at Marcoing, at Battalion Headquarters that I first saw a Yank on active service; he was a Doctor attached to the Regiment.

After completing our mission we returned to Sorel. As we were leaving Marcoing, shells started to fall and as luck would have it we left just before the German counter-attack. They broke through on the right flank of the twenty-ninth Division and reached the Twenty-ninth Division Headquarters at Gouzeaucourt. General de Lisle had to take his papers and beat it on horse-back. The Cavalry saved the day. At the transport line I was standing by with a tin of gas ready to burn all the mail that had accumulated for the past fourteen days. This offensive was the first time so many tanks were used. It was the longest engagement to date and lasted over two weeks. There were 79 killed, 340 wounded and 43 missing.

Sorel was a railhead. The Battalion that was being relieved came here and boarded box cars, used to transport cattle in peacetime, when they got the signal. All in good spirits, we were off leaving the line behind. I had a large backlog of parcel mail and this was put on board. I also had the Christmas cards for the troops. We made ourselves comfortable for the night and when we arrived at Bapaume we could go no further as the railway track had been severed by shellfire or bombing. We all had to disembark and transfer to another train on the other side of the break. My problem was getting the mail across to the other train, which must have been a quarter of a mile away. It was hard going even with all the Regiments helping me. I must have carried about four bags, there were more, across and was just arriving with a bag on my back when someone shouted, "All Aboard!" I wasted no time boarding an open flat car. There were others who were holding packages when they heard the magic words. They dropped everything on the tracks and scrambled aboard. We do not know how long it would be before the train would be moving, but were not taking any chances. The flat car was not as comfortable as the boxcar we were left there with no shelter from the elements. Major Bernard came on the scene and said, "Stacey, all the mail aboard?" What could I say. He knew by time and distance it was impossible to have moved it all and by the look on his face he was joking, so I answered with a smile, "It's all aboard sir." Who should be on the same car with me but Jack Bartlett, Sergeant supervisor of all the Battalion Cooks. He used to make out the daily menus for the troops when out of the line. It was a difficult job with only bully beef, jam, cheese, biscuits and sometimes, which was not very often, bread. Sometimes we would get rolled oats in place of biscuits to make porridge, which we did, in our own canteens, but we would never get any milk or sugar. To cook the porridge we would wrap burlap around a candle and light it. It was something different and warmed us up. Jack and I sat there waiting, expecting at any moment for the train to start. Surveying the heap that was left behind when the "All Aboard" was sounded, I thought it was the best policy to put aboard as much as we could. There was plenty of room on the flat car. There were some bags of Worchester's mail and one box that bore a familiar mark that we had often seen, but could never get too close to. Now, here it was right in our hands and we were the only two aboard. Sure enough, it was what we thought. It contained two one-gallon stone jars marked SRD; that was the code word for rum. Jack, the Sergeant Cook took it, having a better chance to handle it. When we reached our next billets I paid regular visits to Jack with my water bottle to get it filled with some Dutch courage as long as it lasted.

I was told that the Christmas cards were seen blowing around after the railway was bombed. They were printed especially for the Regiment with a caribou head embossed in gold. They were to be given to the boys to send home Christmas greetings. You can guess what happened to the rest of the Christmas parcels.

It was now December and word spread that we would not be paid for Christmas and that was bad news for the troops. I heard that Padre Nangle, who was caterer for Headquarters Officers mess, was going to General Headquarters at Montreuil. I asked him if he would cash a cheque for me there. He said, "Write it out", which I promptly did in the amount of two hundred and fifty francs. He took a wad of notes from his pocket and counted out two hundred and fifty francs and passed them to me. Now, I was in clover again. It was true that our pay did not arrive for Christmas. I had an envied position with my close friends. ❀

chapter twenty four

After the Battle of Cambrai, the Royal Newfoundland Regiment was sent to Humbercourt, a rest area where they spent 12 days.

It was here that Newfoundland Governor Sir Walter Davidson paid his first visit as the Regiment's Honourary Colonel.

Mid-December brought snow which began falling on the 16th and by next day was six inches deep, with heavy drifts in many places.

On the morning of December 18, the Newfoundlanders marched away from Humbermouth with orders to join the Fourth Army in the Hazebrouck area. It was after dark when the men reached Boubers-sur-Canche where they spent the night before continuing another 12 miles to Le Parcq.

On December 20, they reached the village of Fressin where they would celebrate their fourth Christmas away from home.

Memoirs

Blighty and Belgium and it's over.
We were on the march for three days when it began to snow. The orders for

the day were issued the night before. A Division lorry was slated to pick up all the Battalion blankets in the morning and take them to our next stop; this would relieve the boys from having to carry them. The Transport would accompany the Battalion. The general service wagon, a four-wheeled vehicle, was used to carry all the Officer's packs that were Brigade's orders. On the morning before leaving, the CO, Col. Hadow took a walk out on the road to see the conditions for himself as quite a layer of snow had fallen during the night. When he came back, ignoring Brigade's orders, he implemented his own plan and had the Officer's kits removed from the GS wagon and replaced with the men's blankets. The kits were left to be picked up by the Division lorry. After a twelve-mile march we were billeted in the village and everyone was comfortably stowed away for the night with their blankets. The CO of the Essex Regiment came in to see Hadow. He was in a hell of a stew and said his men had no blankets because the lorry was stuck in the snow. "Oh!" said Hadow with a smile, "Our men have their blankets", and then went on to explain what he had done. I had great respect for Hadow. He was a great organizer and always ready to cut clear of red tape.

While at Marcoing I came across a brand new German rifle. Having a mania for souvenirs and knowing that shortly I was going on leave to Blighty I had a good chance to hold on to it. I obtained a holster to put it in so it would be out of sight. After the three-day march we arrived at Fressin, a village not far from Amiens. It was out of bounds for all ranks except Officers and you could not enter it without a pass. We were billeted in a school, which doubled as an orderly room. The schoolmaster and his wife, who lived close by, were very nice people. He could speak a little more English than we could speak French. We were trying to tell him about our Newfoundland climate: how cold it was and how much snow we would get. We could not make him understand about the snow. A thought struck me to go outside and bring in a handful, to their delight. The schoolmaster said to us, "You wait until Marie Louise, our daughter, comes home for Christmas, which won't be long now. She can speak good English". We were all looking forward to seeing Marie Louise. We found out she could speak English, but not ours. It seemed to me like a Grade 2 student reciting. This is what she said, "Consider the lilies of the field how they grow. They toil not, neither do they spin and yet I say unto you that even Solomon in all his glory was not arranged like one of these."

It had been over twelve months since I had been away from the theatre of war and French soil. I heard rumours that leave was about to be given, which happened only when the Battalion was out of the front line or in the quiet sector. You did not know when you were going to get leave until it was published on Battalion's orders. There would not be any more than a half day's notice for you to get a pass. When you did, you would not only be the proud possessor of a pass that was good for fourteen days, but a voucher that would take you to your destination; the address of which you had to give. You were responsible for taking your full equipment, including your rifle. With no Officer in charge you were on your own when you went aboard the leave train at the railhead.

I spent Christmas at Fressin with the boys. As I said before, there was no pay for Christmas. You would have to go through it to realize the feeling. I reached Boulonge on December 30, 1917 and I stayed the night in the rest camp. Here we had a lecture as to the types of souvenirs that we were allowed to take with us on leave. No firearms, bombs or shells of any kind were allowed. If you were caught with any of the "not list" you would lose your leave, be sent back to your unit and stood a good chance of being court marshalled. I had the German rifle in the holster with me, and having held on to it this long, decided to take a chance. The German rifle was a little longer than the short Lee Enfield rifle, so the nozzle projected out of the top of the holster. We moved off to the leave boat at dockside, everyone with a kit bag full. The Red caps could not check everyone, but would pick out an occasional person and search his bag. We had to pass single file down the gangway, which extended for some distance. There were no less than three Military Policemen scrutinizing everyone as they passed: one at the top, one in the middle and one on board the leave ship. I had passed the first two MP's, the other on the boat was not a regular, he was a C3, a member who was classified as being unfit for normal military tasks, but he had a band on his arm marked MP. I was on the boat close to the funnel when he spotted the nozzle of the rifle projecting out of the holster which I had so successfully kept from view when passing the first two MP's. Now I momentarily despaired, to think that I had gotten aboard and was about to be caught. He drew my attention to it. I made all kinds of excuses and said, "what about throwing it overboard." The way he was talking, he was afraid that the other two MP's might have seen it. I edged closer to the ship's funnel to keep out of the sight of the other MP's. As luck would have it, I had a ten-franc note in my pocket. I put the note in the palm of my right hand and said, "How is everyone at home? So glad to see you." I shook hands with him and in doing so placed the ten-franc note in the palm of his hand as I walked off. It worked. While on the boat I kept the rifle at a distance from me in case of any inquiries if so, I did not own it. I found out that it made no difference and I could have hung it around my neck if I wanted. I took it with me when I went home to Watlington, England.

We landed at Southampton, and what a feeling it was coming from the trenches, with trench mud on our boots and puttees and with our bosom friends fresh from France. This was one time when we were proud. We carried our visual discomforts as haughtily as a General, with hopes that we would come out of it all alive, while being constantly aware of what we had been through. The same procedure was followed this time as on my previous leave twelve months earlier. That is, getting my pay at Pay and Records Office, buying a new outfit and passing as a General if I had the stars. Doing what you like is quite a change from Army discipline. However, all these good things came to an end after the fourteen days. We had to go to Waterloo station to catch the train that carried us back. If we were not broke by this time, we were *badly bent. At the station we met others going back to France, but not with a glad eye. Here we met again our leave party, Bill Hibbs and one of our cooks Paddy Stamp. As we were about to pull out, Paddy started kissing all the girls. It did not matter who they were, they might even have some others' wives. On arrival at Southampton, word was around that we would not be leaving until the next day, January 15, 1918. That meant a night in the rest camp where you were given a blanket, bed and Army rations. We did not like this idea because we could not get out for the night. We fell in to go down to the rest camp and as we passed down the main street a few of us old vets, who knew the ropes slipped out of the ranks. We had the evening off and a decent bed to sleep in. We reported early the next morning to the rest camp. My pass was dated from December 30, 1917, to January 13, 1918, which was fourteen days. Staying one night at rest camp delayed me a day, therefore I was one day over my pass. I was supposed to get the rest camp Major to sign my pass for the extra time, but I did not stay at the rest camp for the night and failed to get my pass signed.*

On the same day the Royal Newfoundland Regiment arrived in Frissin, the men bid farewell to Lieutenant-Colonel Hadow, who had commanded the men in eight major operations in Gallopoli, France and Flanders, and was now being invalided home.

His temporary replacement was Lieutenant-Colonel J.R. Meiklejohn.

On New Year's Day, Lieutenant-Colonel J.S. Woodruffe, of the Royal Sussex Regiment, was welcomed as the new commanding officer.

During the first week in January, the Regiment moved northward towards St. Omer. It was here that Jim Stacey rejoined them after a two-week furlough in England.

On arrival at Boulonge I discovered that the Battalion, the main bulk of which had been lodged at Fressin, was on the move again, so after a two-day march we found ourselves in another rest camp at a place called Zudausques, situated about 4 miles west of St. Omer. All three of us, Paddy Stamp, Bill Hibbs and I were broke, so the rest camp was our home for the next four days. We did not have enough money to treat ourselves to a bottle of Vin Blanc in the local cafe. As we sat down to a table one afternoon, low and behold, there on the floor was a ten-franc note. We were in clover for a short while.

The master plan was for the Division to march from Fressin, to an area West of Ypres in Belgium, taking more than six days to do so. We stayed at Zudausques a fortnight and then we were on the march again for another four days. This took us back to the same sector where we had been in 1916 and 1917. We moved into supports at Vlamertinghe and Poperinghe and then back in reserves at Steenvoorde, which was just behind the line, and clear of the shellfire. It was quite a change from Flander's mud. Here we went through the usual procedure of a shower bath. Although the water was scarce but cold, we all had to take part while our clothes were being deloused. This was accomplished by having them steam boiled. Capt. Dick Sheppard was in charge of the delousing outfit. We would then have kit inspection and if we were short of anything it would be issued to us including iron rations, which we were supposed to eat only when told to do so. All shortages were docked from our pay. At the end of the war it is said that some of the vets still owed money to the Regiment because of kit shortages.

When the troops were in the line they had to be fed. Hot food had to be prepared, especially in the winter, behind the lines, over charcoal stoves. The food, which normally consisted of soup or stew, was put in metal containers and placed on a two-wheeled Horse-drawn cart and carried as close as possible to the front line. Parties from various units would then carry the containers of food to the troops. This solution was not always satisfactory as periodically the carriers would come under fire and the soup or skilly would be lost.

During our final stay in reserves at Steenwerck, the Portuguese were holding the line in front of Armentieres. The Germans attacked and broke through and the Regiment had to get aboard lorries to be taken up the line to try to stop the advance. Headquarters and Transport moved off to keep in touch with the Battalion and were billeted in a wood-lined field for the night. The Transport took the rations up to the Battalion and on returning they found a porker pig on the road. It was used eventually to supplement our rations. The civilian refugees that evacuated the villages were coming back in droves as we moved forward. They were sleeping in barns or wherever they found places to lay their heads. We gave them assurances that everything would be all right in a short while, but I'm sure they would not believe us. While we were in this area, a child was born in a hayloft very close to where we camped.

It was soon after this that we had to move out and keep on the move because of the shelling. The next place we camped was well sheltered. It had woods on three sides. We slept in tents and thought it safe, as we had not been shelled for a few days. We found a cow, Bossy, roaming the highway. We tied her to one of the limber wheels. This gave us extra rations, namely, fresh milk for breakfast. All went well until Fritz found us one morning and started to put over HE and incendiary shells. One shell burst very close to us, as I was eating breakfast; so close in fact that when I looked out, what did I see but that our milk supply was finished, for there was Bossie, teats up. The shell had killed her.

I was standing by a pile of blankets when a shell came over and burst on the opposite side. The blankets protected me but a fellow named Hunt, who was about fifty yards away, received a piece of shell in his back. I found out that sometimes, it was safer to be near where the shell burst on the ground than at a distance from it, because the shell pieces normally spread out in an arc. It did not take us long to move from this spot to a quieter one. The villagers had left and their cafes were unattended. With Company post orderlies from the Hants and Worcester Battalions we began to sample the Vin Blanc *and the Vin Rouge that was behind the bar. When one mixes ones drinks, one begins to have a sleepy feeling. That is what happened to me, so I took a snooze behind some trees. I do not know precisely how long I was there but when I awoke the sun was low in the sky. What took my notice was a large number of captive sausage balloons. They were held fast by a hawser attached to a windlass on a truck. I thought at first that they were our own but discovered a short time later that they belonged to the enemy. The town, in which they were located, was Bailleul, about a thousand yards away and in German hands.* ✸

🔲 *chapter twenty five*

When the Royal Newfoundland Regiment left Fressin, they marched northward to Zudausques, a small village four miles west of St. Omer. Here they stayed for two weeks, training with other battalions of the 88th Brigade, which were in rest nearby.

On January 19, the 29th Division took over the front line in the Passchendaele sector. The Royal Newfoundland Regiment, meanwhile, was sent to Brandhoek, four miles west of Ypres, then on to Hasler Camp, where they spent a week working on strengthening defenses to meet an anticipated German offensive in the spring.

On January 26, the Regiment took over part of the front line for a four-day period. Four days later, when they were relieved, the men returned to Brandhoek for further training.

On February 19, the Regiment, its numbers increased by a draft of 173 reinforcements, was sent to Poperinghe. On March 7, the Newfoundlanders returned to the front line as the 29th Division once again took over the sector north of Passchendaele. On the night of March 11, C Company was caught in an enemy bombardment which killed 12 men and wounded 54 more.

During the next three weeks, the Regiment had two more short turns of four and five days in the front line. The rest of the time was divided between Hasler Camp and the billets at Poperinghe. Wherever the men were, the back breaking work of digging and wiring defenses was unending in that Flanders spring of 1918.

On March 21, the Germans launched a major offensive with 71 divisions attacking on a 50-mile front extending from the River Scarpe to the Oise.

Within a week, the Germans had advanced 30 miles.

By the time the offensive was fought to a standstill on April 5, the British and French forces had suffered nearly 250,000 casualties.

On April 9, in what military historians later called the Lys Offensive, the German 6th Army launched an assault on the southern Armentieres front.

By the end of the day, the Germans had opened a hole in the British front 10 miles wide and five miles deep.

The next day the German Fourth Army extended the battle area north.

Straight from the front line trenches at Passchendaele, on their way to Poperinghe for a period of rest, the Royal Newfoundland Regiment, with the rest of the 88th Brigade, was ordered to join the 25th Division for a critical situation which had developed near Bailleul.

A little after 4 p.m. on April 9, the Newfoundlanders arrived in Bailleul and dug in for the night.

The next morning, the Regiment was placed in reserve and the 88th Brigade was put under the command of the 34th Division. At mid-day, on April 11, the Royal Newfoundland Regiment was shifted to a position half a mile north of the Bailleul-Armentieres road in order to protect the 88th Brigade's left flank. Field Marshal Haig issued an order that every position must be held to the last man.

The following day, during a fierce attack, the Monmouthshire Regiment on the left flank of the Newfoundlanders was cut off and suffered heavy casualties. A platoon from C Company. which went to the aid of the Monmouths, was overcome by the Germans and all were either killed or taken prisoner. The rest of C Company fell back and regrouped with the Regiment. A final enemy attack at dusk was halted, and the Regiment, under the covering fire of its Lewis gunners, was able to withdraw.

On the evening of April 13, the Regiment was again engaged in a furious battle which resulted in halting the enemy 25 yards from their position. That night, the 88th Brigade withdrew to a position on the Ravelsberg Ridge. The orderly withdrawal in the entire sector continued until a shorter and more defensible line was established on April 16. The Regiment suffered 176 casualties over this period.

Three Newfoundlanders won the Distinguished Conduct Medal for their gallantry during the battle in front of Bailleul: Sergeant Ernest Gullicksen of Traytown, Sergeant William Haynes of Catalina and Private Thomas Pittman, a St. John's man who was later the model for the statue of the Fighting Newfoundlander in Bowring Park.

The Battle of the Lys continued until the end of the month but the Royal Newfoundland Regiment was not involved in any other major actions.

The Regiment received the Battle Honours "Lys" and "Bailleul" for emblazonment on the Colours for its part in these battles.

On April 21, the Newfoundlanders were relieved in the line by a French regiment and marched to farm billets near Steenvoorde, where they were immediately joined by their 10 per cent reserve.

On April 26, the Royal Newfoundland Regiment was temporarily withdrawn from operations and its services as part of the 29th Division came to an end.

The men went to Etaples for rest, but were shortly moved six miles to Montreuil, where they provided the guard at Sir Douglas Haig's headquarters.

From early May to mid-August, the Royal Newfoundland Regiment continued to furnish the personal bodyguard for Haig and to supply the guards for general headquarters.

During August, veteran members of the Blue Puttees were granted a month's leave to visit family and friends in Newfoundland.

The first draft, numbering 55 men, left for England on July 24.

Heading Home

We were on the move quite a lot until the Battalion was relieved. We were also under strength, as reinforcements were not coming out fast enough to keep the Battalion at full strength. When we were finally relieved, we bid goodbye to the Twenty-ninth Division and the 88th Brigade with whom we had been attached since 1915. While speaking to Hadow at Seven Oaks in 1961 he gave me some information that I did not know at the time. He told me that the Twenty-ninth Division was the most efficient of the British Army. He explained that the Units that comprised the Division were on duty in the near and Far East at the outbreak of the war. Battalions on Foreign Service had to be kept up to full strength and were comprised of regular soldiers with five to seven years' experience. The Battalions on home service comprised 75 percent of regular army personnel and 25 percent of reserves at the outbreak of the war. The Twenty-ninth division units first went into action at Gallipoli. There was only one Battalion that was not made up of regulars and they were the 6th Royal Scots of the 88th Brigade. When we, the Newfoundland regiment, joined the Twenty-ninth Division, we took the place of the 6th Royal Scots. In Warwickshire on the main road between Coventry and London, near Rugby, is a place called Punchurch. It is famous for its beautiful avenue of trees planted in 1921 as a Memorial to the Twenty-ninth Division, which was billeted in the neighborhood before embarking for Gallipoli in 1915.

The Battalion moved to the village of Ecuires, about a mile from Montreuil, which had been the Headquarters of the British Army in France and Belgium. While here we were assigned to guard duty. Montreuil, a quaint, old, walled-in, small, town was the ideal place for General Headquarters. However, one had to have a pass in order to enter. What I distinctly remember were the comings and goings of the motor cycle Dispatch Riders. When they neared a large building one could not help but hear the roar from their exhausts, which seemed like hundreds of typewriters going full blast all at the same time. When we took over the billets at Ecuires we did not have to be told who the previous occupants were, as we could see their trade marks all over the walls. There were all kinds of sketches and paintings. They were a Regiment of artists. I guess it was deemed unrealistic to expose the artists to all the hazards of war so they were put on guard duty at General headquarters. The Household Cavalry also stayed here.

In the billet in which I stayed I came across a plain postcard that had a poem written on both sides, that must have been received by one of the occupants from his girlfriend. Though broken in half I still have the card.

The poem reads as follows:

There is a constant and careful collecting
Of strongest brown paper and twine.
There's a special pen nib for directing,
Free flowing and not over fine.
There's a farsighted skill in packing
For the problem's increasingly great.
Not to leave out anything he's lacking,
And still keep an eye on the weight.
There's a soreness of feminine fingers
For the knots must be terribly tight.
There's a look that half-nervously lingers,
For fear the address isn't right.
There's a trust that the waves will be tender,
That no submarine lurks near the coast,
And a wish in the soul of the sender
That she might be sent Parcel Post.
Oh soldiers whose comforts are meager
When the Corporal sings out your name.
When your hands are schoolboyishly eager,
To seize and examine your claims.
Do you guess at the paper you're tearing?

As the fags in your pockets you shove.
That each parcel from Blighty is bearing
An ocean of love.
— Jessie Pope

Every Friday was market day in Montreuil. On that day the town was full of farmers from the surrounding districts selling their stocks. Everyone appeared jolly. There was one cafe that I occasionally visited where I could get a light lunch and real coffee in a pewter mug. On market day this cafe would be filled with a crowd of jolly farmers who were fond of black coffee. I noticed they would order a mug of coffee, drink half, and fill the mug up with cognac and so on. The process would continue so that the original cup of coffee contained one- percent coffee and 99 percent cognac. By that time they would be happy and singing if they were capable.

Guard duty was not only confined to the ground alone but also the sky. On the wall in an elevated position was a lookout guard, who scanned the skies for planes, using a very long telescope mounted on a tripod. On one occasion, when Sgt. Ches Noseworthy was in charge, I noticed the telescope was not pointing toward the skies but was scanning the surrounding woods. He certainly wasn't looking for planes.

I have a book, titled "The First Five Hundred". It is a short history of the Battalion's war effort and includes the names and lists the decorations awarded for conspicuous bravery and devotion to duty. A visitor who was looking over the list said to me, "I see you won the Military Medal", and he showed me where on the Cambrai list, "A.J. Stacey" was listed as winning the Military Medal. I straightened the matter out for him, for it was not I. There was only one other Stacey in the Regiment up to July 1918 and the most peculiar part was that his initials were "A.J." as well. His first name was Alfred. His regimental number was 1747, whereas mine was 466. I never had a chance to meet him as when we were last in Belgium he was going on leave to Blighty. As he was waiting at the railhead behind the line to take the leave boat to Boulogne, a lone shell came over and killed him. He was the Stacey who won the Military Medal. Later when I was on leave and called at the Pay and Records Office to get my pay book fixed up, Fred Marshall was surprised and said, "Thought you were killed." Such is war.

In July of 1918 we had a visitor all the way from Newfoundland in the person of the Hon. John R. Bennett, Minister of Militia. Through him it was arranged that what was left of the First Five Hundred should go on a month's leave home to Newfoundland. The Conscription Bill was passed in 1917, so from then on new reinforcements would be coming out as fast as they were trained. On July 25th I said goodbye to the Force in France and I did not set foot there again until 1961, when I visited Beaumont Hamel.

We boarded the leave boat at Boulonge and arrived at Winchester, the camp of the 2nd Battalion, the next day. I received a pass and headed for London.

We eventually left England by boarding the S.S. Olympic at Southampton. This was the second trip for me on this great ship. The Olympic had performed a wonderful service in carrying troops to the theatre of war and now she was taking us on what was to be our last trip across the Atlantic. We landed at the Cunard Docks in New York, where we were marched off and we had to wait while the Hon. John R. Bennett went to look for a conveyance to take us to the Grand Central Railway Station. We were left all alone with no Officer of the Regiment in charge. Bennett might have known something about politics, but he knew nothing whatever about handling old vets with about four years active service. We waited half an hour for his return. What would you expect us to do, stand there and wait in New York city where before even smaller towns were out of bounds? I started to look around and explore the surroundings. To Bennett's grief, most found taverns. You know the result. The upshot was some returned in wheelbarrows and any other means of conveyance. As a matter of fact, I think some were left behind. Bennett learned a lesson.

When we arrived at North Sydney, Nova Scotia, he would not let us out of his sight while we waited for the S.S. Kyle to arrive to take us to St. John's. To me the S.S. Kyle was quite different from the S.S. Olympic but I am no sailor. They kept us sailing around for two hours outside St. John's Harbour in a rough sea until the official party was all ready to give us a hero's welcome. We landed August 4, 1918, on a months leave just four years after the outbreak of World War I. When we reported back in September, the flu was prevalent, and this prevented us from leaving. We never left as the war ended shortly afterwards.

For the Blue Puttees, the month's leave in Newfoundland passed all too quickly.

Before the time came for them to re-cross the Atlantic, Governor Harris was presented with a petition containing almost 5,000 names which asked that the boys who had already spent four winters overseas be extended furlough until the spring of 1919.

The request, as far as the Blue Puttees were concerned, was granted.

The proposal of furlough for others was, however, turned down. ⊛

Thomas R. (Tommy) Ricketts (1901-1967).
Enlisted at age 15. His actions in clearing a
German gun battery on Oct. 4, 1918, led to his
receiving the Victoria Cross,
the highest British military honour.
(courtesy The Trail of the Caribou)

 chapter twenty six

In eastern Europe, the early part of 1918 was marked by Russia's withdrawal from the war.

In March of 1917, a popular uprising against Russia's imperial government had resulted in the abdication of Czar Nicholas and the establishment of a provisional government which continued the war against the Central Powers.

However, when the Bolshevik party seized power through a military coup, a key point of their policy was the withdrawal of Russia from the war. On December 15, an armistice was signed between the Russians and Austro-German negotiators and fighting ceased on the Eastern front.

Russian losses in the First World War were horrendous. Total casualties numbered a staggering 9,150,000 men. Of those, 1,700,000 men were killed or died. Russia's casualties in the First World War were greater than those sustained by any army in any previous war.

The Americans entered the war in April, 1917 under the command of General John Joseph Pershing. By June, 1917, more than 175,000 American troops were training in France, and one division was in the lines of the Allied sector near Belfort.

By November, 1918, nearly 2,000,000 American troops were in Europe.

At the beginning of 1918, the Germans, realizing that victory by means of submarine warfare was impossible and that they must force a decision on the Western Front before American troops may take up positions there in force, planned an all-out spring attack to break through the Allied lines and reach Paris.

The opening drive of their powerful offensive began March 21 and was directed at the British front south of Arras. The drive pushed the British back 40 miles before it was halted, on April 5, by hastily summoned French reserves.

During April, a second German thrust took Messines Ridge and Armentieres from the British.

In June, a powerful German surprise attack against the French on the Aisne enabled the Germans to reach a point of the Marne only 37 miles from Paris.

The Americans, going into battle in force for the first time, and the French managed to halt the German advance.

The Germans advanced further in June, but by the middle of July the force of their offensive had largely been spent. In the Second Battle of the Marne, they succeeded in crossing the river, but once they were across their advance was stopped by French and American troops. The attack drove the Germans back over the Marne and marked the Allies taking an initiative on the Western Front that they retained to the end of the war.

Beginning with a British drive (August 8-11) into the German lines around Amiens, the Allies began the offensive that resulted in German capitulation three months later.

In early September, 1918, members of the Royal Newfoundland Regiment overseas were ready for action and fit to play a part in what would be the final offensives of the war. The Regiment was now part of the 28th Infantry Brigade, of the 9th Scottish Division. On September 19, the Newfoundlanders, with a full complement of officers and a strength of 724 other ranks, relieved a battalion of the 26th Brigade in the front trenches at Ypres.

At dawn on September 28, with the 2nd Royal Scots Fusiliers on the left and the 9th Scottish Rifles on the right, the Newfoundlanders advanced on their first objective, Polygon Wood, in a creeping barrage. By midday, the men were at Polygon Wood, having advanced three miles at a cost of 15 casualties.

The following day, the advance continued successfully to the Keiberg Ridge and on to the village of Keiberg. Since the battle began on September 28, the Newfoundlanders had advanced a distance of nine miles, during which their casualties had numbered a little over 100.

The fighting on September 29 brought the Regiment 12 major decorations for bravery.

Next day, the weary troops marched back a few miles to some ruined houses in the vicinity of Keiberg, where they were to have a day's rest. The Newfoundlanders' stay in reserve lasted until the night of October 2, when they again moved up to the front line. The previous day, an attack by the 27th Brigade had driven the enemy out of Lederghem, but without support the village could not be held. The sector which the Royal Newfoundland Regiment took over included Lederghem station and some 500 yards of the railway track along the west side of town, which they defended until they were relieved on the night of October 6/7.

The attack resumed on October 14 with zero hour set for 5:35 a.m. The evening before the attack the men began moving into position along the railway track north of Lederghem. The advance began under a barrage of shrapnel and thick smoke fired by field guns only 200 yards behind the infantry. The heavy concentration of smoke combined with a thick ground mist to produce a dense fog which made it almost impossible to keep on the line but resulted in the surprise capture of many enemy prisoners.

After a difficult crossing of the Wulfdambeek river, the Newfoundlanders ended up pinned down by enemy shelling from a well-defended German battery.

The men were facing annihilation when Private Thomas Ricketts, a 17-year-old from Middle Arm, White Bay, who had lied about his age in 1916 in order to join the Regiment, volunteered to go forward with his section commander and a Lewis gun to attempt to capture the battery. What took place then was described in the following extract from the London Gazette of January 6, 1919.

Advancing by short rushes under heavy fire from enemy machine guns with the hostile battery, their ammunition was exhausted when still 300 yards from the battery.

The enemy, seeing an opportunity to get their field guns away, began to bring up gun teams. Private Ricketts, at once realizing the situation, doubled back 100 yards under the heaviest machine gun fire, procured further ammunition, and dashed back to the Lewis gun, and by very accurate fire drove the enemy and the gun teams into a farm.

His platoon then advanced without casualties, and captured the four field guns, four machine guns and eight prisoners.

A fifth field gun was subsequently intercepted by fire and captured.

By his presence of mind in anticipating the enemy intentions and his utter disregard of personal safety, Private Ricketts secured the further supply of ammunition which directly resulted in these important captures and undoubtedly saved many lives. [38]

Tommy Ricketts first saw action at the Steenbeek River. He received a bullet in the right leg at Marcoing and rejoined the Regiment in time for the fighting at Balleul.

His heroic action near the Wulfdambeek River resulted in his becoming the youngest winner of the Victoria Cross in the British Army. The only other Newfoundlander to win the Victoria Cross in the First World War was Private John Bernard Croak from Little Bay, who served with the 13th Battalion, Canadian Expeditionary Force. Croak won his honour for his actions on August 8, 1918, during the opening stage of the Battle of Ameins.

After Ricketts brave move, the Regiment advanced to the Steenbeck before digging in for the night.

The day's advance of three miles had placed the 28th Brigade further east than any other troops of the Second Army. For the Royal Newfoundland Regiment, it was a very successful day. There was a count of 500 prisoners, 94 machine guns, five field guns, three other guns and vast supplies of ammunition.

The operation was a success but the cost in human life was heavy. At dawn on October 15, the Regiment could muster only 300 men. The following day, the Regiment marched to St. Catherine Cappelle, a village three miles north of Courtrai, and just west of the railway. On the night of October 19, the Newfoundlanders crossed the river Lys, with orders to take the village of Vichte and to push on towards the Scheldt River.

Under heavy enemy fire, the best they could do was capture the railway station and gain a foothold in the western outskirts of Vichte. They were relieved on October 21. Three days later, with the 9th Division, the Newfoundlanders went forward in what turned out to be the final attack of the war.

The first objective was a German held ridge which formed the last barrier before the Scheldt River.

The attack ended within sight of the Scheldt when orders came to consolidate and defend the ground already taken.

Plans were made for a forced crossing of the Scheldt on November 11, but the signing of an Armistice ending the war made this unnecessary.

For their role in the advance from Ypres to the Scheldt, the Royal Newfoundland Regiment was granted the Battle Honours "Ypres 1918" and "Courtrai" for emblazonment on the Colours.

The final Battle Honours awarded to the Royal Newfoundland Regiment were "France and Flanders 1916-1918." ✳

chapter twenty seven

When Jim Stacey and other members of the Royal Newfoundland Regiment returned to Newfoundland for a month's leave on August 8, 1918, they had no way of knowing the war would soon be over.

In July, not long before Jim arrived back in St. John's, there was a parade and concert which paid tribute to the "noble fellows who had fallen in the drive July 1, 1916."

The Royal Newfoundland Regiment's Captain Keegan was quoted in The Evening Telegram as saying those who died had handed down the "grandest of traditions, which must be kept up to the end."

The day after the parade the paper reported there had been An Oversight.

What had happened was that Private James Moore of Duckworth Street, a Blue Puttee described as having "left two feet in Europe and has now to cripple around on artificial legs and crutches" had been inadvertently left out of the parade and subsequent celebrations at Government House.

Moore had been wounded three times, in Gallipoli, again on July 1 and a third time in October 1916. On the day of the parade, he was at home dressed and waiting for someone to come pick him and take him to the celebrations. but for whatever reason he was missed.

On July 4, The Evening Telegram carried a death notice for a "Beaumont Hamel Hero" who had died the previous day.

Private Gregory Neville, age 22, was wounded on July 1, 1916. He spent time in hospital in London, before being shipping home and dying of complications at Jensen Camp Hospital in St. John's.

The young man was listed as the only son of Patrick Neville of Topsail.

Along with the death notice there were two In Memoriams. One was for Sergeant John French, killed on July 1, 1916. The other was for Private Samuel Learning, who was wounded July 1, and died three days later.

Included in July 4 news: General Haig was celebrating his 57th birthday. The Germans desired a speedy peace with honour. More than two million American troops would be on French soil in six months.

On July 6, the paper carried an entreaty to Newfoundlanders to buy Victory Bonds at 6.5 per cent interest. The bonds were promoted as, "the only thing that stands between the Germans and you."

On July 22, it was reported that about 20,000 of General Pershing's American troops were fighting with the French in an offensive in the Aisne-Marne district.

During July and August, there were advertisements offering a reminder that even with a war on the routine of daily life continued.

On July 25, F. McNamara of Queen Street announced the pending arrival of new American cabbage, Texas silver peel onions, and California oranges, as well as 25-pound boxes of evaporated peaches and apricots.

On August 1, the firm of S. E. Garland promoted the arrival of Zane Grey's novels.

During August, it became increasingly apparent the war was not going well for the Germans. They were reported to be retreating on a number of fronts.

Over the Somme battle front, from the region of Arras to the north of Solassons, the Germans were meeting with defeats which appeared to spell disaster.

On August 17, Mr. Bhattacharji, an Indian astrologer in Calcutta, predicted the war would end on September 5, 1919.

The big news on August 27 was that Germany had given Turkey £10 million and a promise of huge territorial possessions for coming into the war on the side of the Central Powers.

On September 24, it was reported that the Allied advance was continuing on all fronts.

One day, not long after he arrived back in St. John's, Jim Stacey was invited to dinner at the home of a fellow member of the Regiment.

Corporal John Hillier, one of the famous ten credited with saving the French town of Monchy-le-Preux in 1917, lived with his widowed mother on Warbury Street.

His mother, Elizabeth Cassidy, grew up in Frogmarsh, Brigus, and moved to St. John's following her marriage to George Hillier of New Harbour, Trinity Bay. They lived first on Sudbury Street and were in the process of building a new house on Warbury Street when George died unexpectedly on June 8, 1911, leaving behind a wife and seven children.

Following his father's death, John, as the eldest son, took over construction of the two-storey house on Warbury Street, which was known then as Western Avenue.

On the night he was invited to the Hillier home for a dinner of roast beef and Yorkshire pudding, in recognition of his British roots, Jim was introduced to two of John's sisters, Blanche and Elsie.

Jim was intrigued to learn that brown-haired, soft spoken Blanche, who worked as a seamstress at the Water Street firm of Ayre & Sons, had a sweetheart who'd been killed overseas.

She and Lance-Corporal Chesley James Gough, who was killed at Gueudencourt on October 12, 1916, had corresponded regularly up until the time of his death. Gough's letters, bound with a black ribbon, were tucked away in the bottom of the wooden trunk she used as her hope chest.

Jim and Blanche soon began a relationship that started as friendship and was to develop into something much more serious.

By October, 1918, there was no doubt the war was not going in Germany's favour.

On October 1, The Evening Telegram reported that Bulgaria's surrender was complete.

On October 3, there was word the Germans were retreating as Haig's men swept through the Hindenburg Line.

"The white flag is hoisted...Plea of peace from Germany," read an October 7 headline.

"Germans in full retreat," was the headline on October 11.

On October 12, it was reported that Turkey had surrendered and the German retreat homeward was continuing.

On October 15, the Allies refused Germany's peace offer and demanded an unconditional surrender.

The following day, important news was that Spanish Influenza was spreading in Canada and that 153 people had died in Montreal.

On October 17, the Germans were reported retreating from Belgium.

That same day, alarms about Spanish Influenza began appearing in St. John's papers.

"The Spanish Influenza may attack you," warned the firm of Henry Blair.

People were advised to protect themselves against colds with "reliable Canadian made rubbers and overshoes."

The James Baird firm urged using hydrogen peroxide to gargle morning, noon and night.

"Take no chance. Use every precaution to combat the Spanish Flu," read their advertisement.

There were notices to outport magistrates that Spanish Influenza was very contagious.

Magistrates were told to prohibit any unnecessary gathering of people but to avoid panic.

On October 17, The Evening Telegram carried a notice from N.S. Fraser, acting medical officer of health, announcing that because of the influenza epidemic all places of public gathering such as schools, theatres, moving picture and concert halls, would be closed.

Next day, Fraser said all city churches would be closed until further notice.

On October 13, Spanish Influenza was reported on Newfoundland's west coast.

On October 19, the Belgian flag was reported flying over the re-conquered coast.

On October 21, news was that the Germans were leaving France and Belgium.

American president Woodrow Wilson suggested an Armistice on October 24.

On November 2, Turkey signed an Armistice.

On November 5, British, French and American troops were reported engaged in a deep struggle with the Germans that was thought could well be the deciding action of the war.

On November 7, it was announced that hostilities had ceased and an Armistice with Germany had been signed.

The following day, there was word that the Armistice had not yet been signed.

A casualty list published in The Evening Telegram on November 8 contained the names of Sergeant Edward Monohan of the South Side, Private Henry Horwood of Moreton's Harbour, Private John Russell of Bay Roberts, as well as Private Michael O' Brien of Witless Bay, and Sergeant James Newton of Bell Island, who had both been killed on October 25.

On November 11, the paper ran a huge headline: "Germany has surrendered. The war ended at 11 o'clock this morning, Paris time."

Under the headline was a less than flattering reference to German emperor William: "The murderer of Potsdam flees to Holland."

"The world rejoices: Peace accomplished through victory," read a November 12 headline.

With Germany's signing of 35 conditions, surrender was seen as "absolute and unparalleled in history"

There was much rejoicing in Newfoundland when the war was over and the Allies had won.

On November 12, The Evening Telegram reported a "Monster Peace Procession" took place in St. John's. "Regiments, Brigades, Societies, and citizens parade–Bands, Banner, Autos, Carriages in Line–Joy Bells ring out the message of peace at noon. Our gallant ally. La Belle France, represented."

Leading and ending the parade were cars filled with wounded Blue Puttees.

Approximately 12,000 people took part in the parade and another 5,000 followed behind

The parade ended with a ceremony at Government House.

The following day the Blue Puttees held a second parade in St. John's. In what the Telegram called "the second city of Harbour Grace" there was yet another victory celebration which lasted from 3 p.m. Monday until midnight Tuesday. ✹

Postcards common during the First World War (courtesy The Trail of the Caribou)

🔲 *chapter twenty eight*

On November 11, the German Grand Fleet consisting of nine battleships, five battle cruisers, seven light cruisers and 50 destroyers, surrendered.

Germany had a new government in place on November 16.

On November 28, The Evening Telegram reported the Germans had released 1.5 million prisoners of war of all nationalities.

It was reported as well that Spanish Influenza had taken a greater toll of life in the Bay of Islands than four years of war. Worldwide, Spanish Influenza, the most destructive epidemic of modern times, is estimated to have caused 20 million deaths in 1918. In the Bay of Islands area, the deadly flu killed 40 people.

A November 29 article referred to the Germans as "a people past shame," and continued, "We have now no trust whatever in the Germans generally or, strange to say, in a single individual German."

A November 30 headline read: "William found guilty. Germany must pay full cost of war."

The Treaty of Versailles, the peace treaty signed at the end of the First

World War between Germany and the Allies, was negotiated during the Paris Peace Conference held in Versailles beginning January 18, 1919.

Represented at the conference were the United States, Great Britain, France, and Italy.

The German Republic, which had replaced the imperial German government at the end of the war, was prohibited from the parley.

The treaty ending the war contained the establishing covenant for the League of Nations, history's first worldwide peace keeping body.

The treaty detailed the disarmament of Germany and the reparations to be made by her, and provided for post war territorial adjustments on the European continent and in Germany's colonial empire. According to the terms of the Treaty of Versailles, Germany was required to abolish compulsory universal military service; to reduce her army to 96,000 men and 4,000 officers recruited by voluntary enlistment; to demilitarize all the territory on the left bank of the Rhine River and to a depth of 93 miles on the right bank and to stop all importation, exportation and nearly all production of war material. The German navy was limited to six battleships, six light cruisers, 12 torpedo boats, and zero submarines, naval personnel was not to exceed 15,000 officers and men; and all military and naval aviation was to be abandoned by October 1, 1919.

Germany was also required to make extensive financial reparations for damage incurred by the Allied powers during the war. The amount of reparation due and the arrangements for payment by Germany were finally fixed in May, 1919, by an Allied commission.

The total indebtedness was set at $33,000,000,000.

Germany was to repay $500,000,000 annually, plus 26 per cent of the value of its exports.

The First World War raged for four years, three months and 14 days.

It was ended with the signing of an Armistice on November 11, 1918.

The total number of Allied casualties in the land force was 22, 089,709, of whom more than five million died.

The total number of casualties in the land force on the enemy side was 15,404,477, of whom almost four million died.

Deaths among the civilian population caused indirectly by the war were approximately 10 million.

With the war over the nations involved took stock. Among them, they had lost almost twenty million lives. Twenty-one million more had been wounded and, of those, a large number were so badly gassed or maimed that they would be invalids for life. ✸

◼ *chapter twenty nine*

Late in April, 1919, the 1st Newfoundland Battalion joined the Second (Reserve) Battalion at Hazely Downs Camp in England.

A large draft of Newfoundlanders sailed for home in May and others soon followed.

Before the summer of 1919 was over, the majority of the troops had returned to civilian life.

On August 26, the Royal Newfoundland Regiment's 1st Battalion and 2nd Reserve Battalion and the Newfoundland Forestry Corps were officially disbanded.

A week later the Discharge Depot in St. John's was closed, and the office of the District Officer Commander ceased to exist.

The Great War was over. The war that was supposed to end all wars had been won.

But what a terrible toll in human life it had extracted.

Newfoundland's population in 1914 was 263,000.

When the war began and Great Britain issued a cry for help, 12,426 Newfoundlanders offered themselves for service.

Those who enlisted included 2,953 sailors and 500 foresters.

Of all of those who enlisted, 6,179 were accepted into the Newfoundland Regiment, and another 62 joined in Great Britain.

The Newfoundland Regiment sent 1,178 members to Gallipoli.

Many of those who were in Gallipoli, along with 4,213 others, fought in France and Belgium.

The Newfoundland Regiment suffered 1,305 killed and 2,134 wounded.

Of 180 men taken prisoner, 34 died in enemy hands.

Of the more than 6,000 Newfoundlanders who served in the Newfoundland Regiment during the course of the First World War one in five was killed.

The cost of the First World War in terms of lives lost and pain and suffering is immeasurable.

In economic terms, the financial cost of the war to Newfoundland was $16 million, or $64 per head. ⚙

Opening of the War Memorial in St. John's July 1, 1924 (courtesy The Trail of the Caribou)

 chapter thirty

A bronze caribou, the symbol of the Royal Newfoundland Regiment, stands in each of Newfoundland's five battlefield parks in Europe.

At Beaumont Hamel, from a mound 50 feet above St. John's Road, the caribou looks out over the sloping ground, its head pointing to the Danger Tree and the Y Ravine beyond.

At Gueudecourt, the caribou memorial, which is clearly visible from the main Albert-Cambrai road, marks the point of the Regiment's farthest advance on October, 12, 1916.

The memorial commemorating the Regiment's defense of the Marcoing-Masnnieres bridgehead, in the 1917 Battle of Cambrai, is on the Albert-Cambrai road just outside Masnieres.

The caribou at Monchy-le-Preux stands above the ruins of a German concrete strongpoint in the village.

The only Newfoundland memorial to be erected in Belgium is that at Courtrai, located near the place where the River Lys was crossed during the final advance of the war.

In St. John's, there is a sixth caribou in Bowring Park with a plaque nearby that reads:

This replica of the Newfoundland War Memorial on the battlefields of France and Flanders was presented to the city of St. John's by Major William Howe Greene, OBE, in memory of old friends and comrades of the Royal Newfoundland Regiment and was unveiled by Tasker Cook, Mayor of St. John's on 1st July, 1928.

On the other side of the mound there is a metal cross with the dates 1914-1919, and a list of battle names that echo through the years: Armentirers, Passchendaele, Ledeghem, Courtrai, Harlebeke, Suvla, Beaumont Hamel, Gueudecourt, Monchy-Le-Preux, Ypres, Steenbeck, Brombeek, Masnieres.

English sculptor Basil Gotto created the caribou memorials as well as the Fighting Newfoundlander which stands on a hill high above the caribou in Bowring Park.

The Fighting Newfoundlander is a life-sized replica of a soldier in fighting gear poised and ready to throw a Mills bomb. The model for the sculpture was the Royal Newfoundland Regiment's Corporal Thomas Pittman, a St. John's man who won both the Distinguished Conduct Medal and the Military Medal.

The National War Memorial, which was unveiled by Field-Marshal Earl Haig, former Commander-in-Chief of the British forces in France, on July 1, 1924, overlooks St. John's Harbour.

The money to erect the monument was raised by selling $1 shares in the Newfoundland War Memorial Company Unlimited. No one worked harder selling the shares than Father Tom Nangle, the Royal Newfoundland Regiment's overseas padre.

As director of Graves Registration and Enquiry and Newfoundland's representative on the Imperial War Graves Commission, Lieutenant Colonel Nangle also negotiated with some 250 French landowners for the purchase of the park site at Beaumont Hamel and played a leading role in planning and supervising the erection of all the Newfoundland battle memorials and the selection and development of the parks in which they stand.

The monument in St. John's, which was unveiled on the eighth anniversary of the battle of Beaumont Hamel, depicts a female figure symbolizing the spirit of Newfoundland and holding both a torch and a sword.

She is flanked at the lower level by a figure of a soldier of the Royal Newfoundland Regiment and a sailor of the Royal Naval Reserve.

Centered between these two figures is a representative of the Newfoundland Mercantile Marine and the Forestry Corps.

The plaque on the Duckworth Street side of the monument, says,

To the glory of God and in perpetual remembrance of one hundred and ninety-two men of the Newfoundland Royal Naval Reserve, thirteen hundred men of the Royal Newfoundland Regiment, one hundred and seventeen men of the Newfoundland Mercantile Marine and of all those Newfoundlanders of other units of His Majesty's or Allied Forces who gave their lives by sea and land for the defense of the British Empire in the Great War 1914-1918.

For enduring witness also to the services of the men of this island who, during that war, fought, not without honour, in the navies and armies of their empire.

Let them give glory to the Lord and declare his praise to the islands. Isaish 42.10.

A year after he unveiled the memorial in St. John's, Haig officially opened Beaumont Hamel Park in France and unveiled its imposing memorial.

Among those who participated in the ceremony on June 7, 1925, were Marshal Fayolle, Chief of the French General Staff; Newfoundland's Colonial Secretary, J. R. Bennett; Lieutenant-Generals Sir Aylmer Hunter-Weston and Sir Beauvoir de Lisle, and Major-General D.E. Cayley, under whom the Newfoundlanders had fought as members of the 29th Division.

The Royal Newfoundland Regiment was represented by several members, including two former commanding officers, Lieutenant-Colonels A. L. Hadow and A. E. Bernard.

Haig commended the selection of Beaumont Hamel as the site of the principal memorial to Newfoundlanders who had fought in the First World War. He referred to the site as a place "where courage, devotion, and self-sacrifice were poured out, as it seemed at the moment, for no purpose."and said: "You have chosen a scene which, in July, 1916, seemed to many remarkable for the failure of British arms."

Pausing briefly, he went on to praise the fighting spirit which had finally resulted in triumph and concluded by emphasizing the link now forged with France.

This spot will become a place of pilgrimage which, generation after generation, will draw Newfoundlanders to France; which will bring them on their way hither to the shores of England, and by the undying memories it evokes, will keep green among you and us and the people of France the knowledge of the ideals we share, and of the responsibility which is laid upon us by our dead for the future peace and happiness of the world. [39]

At Beaumont Hamel, cast iron plaques below the caribou bear the names of 591 men of the Royal Newfoundland Regiment who died in the Great War and whose graves are not known.

Of those, 139 died on July 1, 1916.

Also commemorated on the panels are 114 men of the Newfoundland Royal Naval Reserve and 115 of the Newfoundland Mercantile Marine.

Among those whose names appear on the memorial register are men from communities all over Newfoundland: From St. John's, Harbour Grace, Bonavista, Harbour Main, Fogo, Twillingate, Change Islands, Moreton's Harbour, Heart's Content, Trinity, St. Barbe, St. Georges and Isle aux Mort.

The memorial lists the names of Captain Eric Ayre, his only brother, Captain Bernard Ayre, and their cousins, Lieutenants Gerald and Wilfrid Ayre, all of whom were killed on July 1. Three of the Ayres died within yards of each other on Hawthorn Ridge, the other fell at Maricourt, in the southern sector of the Battle of Beaumont Hamel.

In 1919, the Postmaster General in St. John's issued a set of twelve stamps in denominations ranging from 1 to 36 cents and depicting a caribou head against a background of misty Newfoundland hills.

Four of the stamps were dedicated to the Royal Naval Reserve, the remainder carried the legend "Trail of the Caribou" together with the names of a place where the Royal Newfoundland Regiment had fought with distinction: Suvla, Gueudecourt, Beaumont Hamel, Monchy, Steenbeck, Longemarche, Cambrai and Combles, commemorating the action at Sailly-Saillisel. ✹

Blanche (Hillier) Stacey, shortly before she and Jim were married.

Jim and his first born child, Ruth, around 1924.

Jim Stacey in England, around 1910.

'Ingleside' in Goulds, the Stacey family home.

Jim and Blanche with 7 of their 12 children, around 1944. Back row: Blanche, Robert, Jim, Betty, Ethel. Front: Janet, Cecil, Harold and Peter. Missing from photo: Ruth, Bruce, George, Ralph, Eleanor.

First World War veterans who went to Beaumont Hamel with Premier Joseph Smallwood in 1961.
Jim is in the front row, second from left, next to Smallwood.

Blanche and Jim Stacey, Goulds, around 1962.

A.J. Stacey and his dog, Buck, taken by his
son, Peter, in 1967. Photo was taken by
the old barn next to the family home
in the Goulds.

▓ *chapter thirty one*

Anthony James Stacey and Blanche Mildred Hillier were married at Wesley United Church in St. John's on September 22, 1920. Their marriage certificate (Number 422) is signed by Reverend Bugden, the officiating minister and witnesses Charlie Stacey, Jim's brother, as well as Florence and John Hillier, Blanche's sister and brother.

A number of years later, they bought a house on 141 Casey Street and began raising a family which eventually grew to include 12 children: Ruth, Bruce, George, Ralph, Eleanor, Betty, Robert, Ethel, Cecil, Peter, Harold and Janet.

For a number of years, Jim owned and operated two restaurants, one on Duckworth Street, the other on Gower Street. As well, he had a mobile van equipped with cooking facilities from which he sold fish and chips, wrapped in newspaper English style, at locations all over St. John's. Older folks in St. John's say their mouths still water when they recall what was for many of them a regular Friday treat. There are some who say that Jim was the first to bring fish and chips to Newfoundland. One of his regular venues was the annual summer Regatta at Quidi Vidi

Lake, in a spot not far from where he and his fellow Blue Puttees underwent training in the summer of 1914. Another of his regular sites was on Duckworth Street, just up the road from the National War Memorial, the monument commemorating all those who died in the long and bloody First World War.

In 1936, Jim and Blanche moved their still growing family from the city into the country, to the Goulds, a distance of about eight miles from St. John's, where they had bought a house on a large tract of land bordering Fourth Pond. Jim then concentrated on farming. He raised chickens and sold their eggs to customers in St. John's. He was as well one of the pioneers in the savoury business. He not only grew and dried the pungent green herb which is a must for any bread stuffing in Newfoundland, he was also among the first to offer savoury for sale in small cellophane packages.

For Jim, the First World War was a grand and glorious adventure he never tired of talking about.

In October, 1954, on the 40th anniversary of the departure of the First 500 from St. John's, Jim and nearly 100 of the 239 surviving Blue Puttees got together in St. John's to mark the occasion.

On October 3, the veterans assembled at the memorial on the old Pleasantville site with a Guard of Honour from the Royal Newfoundland Regiment under the command of Major Wick Collins, Officer Commanding Headquarters Company.

The Regiment's Honourary Lieutenant-Colonel, Major Bert Butler, delivered an address of remembrance and dedication before laying a wreath for fallen comrades.

Afterwards, the poignant sound of the Last Post, blown by a bugler from the Regiment, echoed across nearby Quidi Vidi Lake on the banks of which so many years ago the young and eager First 500 had prepared for a war that was more horrible than they could have dreamed possible.

On the evening of October 3, the veterans heard a sermon preached at Gower Street United Church by the Reverend Stenlake, who had served as padre with the Regiment in France.

The highlight of the anniversary celebrations was a dinner held October 4, where a toast to Absent Comrades was proposed by Padre Stenlake and drank in solemn silence.

Following dinner, the Blue Puttees sang old favourites familiar from those long ago days in England Scotland, Egypt, Gallipoli, France and Belgium.

Seven years later, on July 1, 1961, when a commemorative plaque was unveiled at Beaumont Hamel, among the dignitaries in attendance were ten survivors of the Battle of Beaumont Hamel.

Jim Stacey was there, as were Ernest Aitken of Deer Lake; Howard Morry from Ferryland; Neil Patrick, Corner Brook; Victor Taylor, St.

John's; Roy Spencer, Fortune; Joe and Ken Goodyear from Grand Falls; Sydney Frost of Toronto; and Fred Waterman from Edinburgh. [40]

On July 2, 1969, Jim died suddenly of a heart attack at age 78. Following her husband's death, Blanche sold the property in the Goulds and moved into a seniors' complex in St. John's. She died in 1979, shortly before her 80th birthday. ✸

FOOTNOTES

1. Colonel Gerald Nichlson, The Fighting Newfoundlander, page 116
2. Ibid, page 100
3. Ibid, page 102
4. Ibid, page 120
5. Ibid, Page 131
6. Nicholson, page 211 and the Encyclopedia of Newfoundland and Labrador, Volume , page 177
7. Nicholson, page 213
8. Ibid, page 219
9. Mayo Lind Letters, page 66
10. Nicholson, page 173
11. Mayo Lind Letters, page 89
12. Ibid, page 89
13. R.H. Tait, Newfoundland, page 197
14. Nicholson, page 180
15. John Gallishaw, Trenching at Gallipoli, page 66
16. Letters of Mayo Lind, page 123
17. Nicholson, page 231
18. Ibid, pge 233
19. Joy Cave, What Became of Corporal PIttman, page 95
20. Ibid, page 239
21. Ibid, page 261
22. Mayo Lind Letters, page 161
23. Owen Steele Journal (Centre for Newfoundalnd Studies Archives)
24. Cave, page 11
25. Nicholson, pages 265-266
26. Nicholson, page 281
27. Ibid, page 284
28. Ibid, page 285
29. Funk and Wagnalls and Encyclopedia of Newfoundland and Labrador
30. Cave, pages 74-77
31. Nicholson, page 321
32. Ibid, pages 336 to 338
33. Ibid, pages 339 to 361
34. Ibid, page 431
35. Ibid, page 397
37. Ibid, pages 421-425
38. Ibid, page 518
40. Ibid, pages 527,533

SOURCES

Murphy, Tony and Paul Kenney, The Trail of the Caribou, Harry Cuff Publications (1991)

Nicholson, Colonel Gerald, The Fighting Newfoundlander, Government of Newfoundland

Fardy, Bernard D, Before Beaumont Hamel, Creative Publishers (1995)

Cave, Joy B, What Became of Corporal Pittman, Breakwater Books Ltd. (1976)

The Encyclopedia of Newfoundland and Labrador

Trenching at Gallipoli, John Gallishaw, The Century Company (1916)

The Letters of Mayo Lind, Robinson & Company Ltd. 1919 (Centre for Newfoundland Studies)

Journal of Owen Steele, Centre for Newfoundland Studies Archives, Memorial University

Newspapers: The Evening Telegram and The Daily News

Canada and the First World War, John Swettenham, (The Ryerson Press. 1969

THE FIRST CONTINGENT

On Oct. 4, 1914, the first contingent of the Newfoundland Regiment boarded the SS Florizel in St. John's Harbour enroute for England. Colonel W.H. Franklin, the regiment's commanding officer, had left for England two days earlier. The 20 officers who left Newfoundland with the first contingent were: Norman Harvey Alderdice; Conn Alexander; Charles Robert Ayre; Adolph Ernest Bernard; Bertram Butler; George Thomas Carty; William Hodgson Franklin; Hubert H. Goodridge. James Allan Ledingham; John Wesley March; Joe Nunns; Augustus O'Brien; Lamont Paterson; Arthur Raley; Walter Frederick Rendell; Reginald S. Rowsell; Michael Francis Summers; Robert Holland Tait; Henry Alfred Timewell; Arthur William Wakefield; Charles Whighton. The others who left on Oct. 4 were: Jacob Abbott (regimental number 168); Stanley Abbott (283); Thomas Wilfred Allan (263); William Anderson (418); John Donald Andrews (315); Ralph Martin Andrews (55); Archibald Ash (575); Wilfred Douglas Ayre (164), killed in action July 1, 1916; Laurie Graham Baine (592); Lawrence Barnes (528), killed in action Aug. 14, 1917; Thomas Frank Barron (568); Oswald Knight Batstone (227); Leonard Josiah Barrett (372); Rupert Wilfred Bartlett, (166) killed in action Nov. 30, 1917; William Washer Bartlett, ((270) died of wounds March, 1917; Chesley Charles Belbin (167); John Alexander Rendell (207), killed in action Oct. 9, 1917; Dominici Bennett (245); Frank Bennett (284); Frank Gordon Best (42), killed in action Oct. 9, 1917; Alexander Bishop (57); Elijah Bishop (597); Henry Bishop (291)' Samson Bixby; Herbert Blackall (448); Michael Blyde (280) died of wounds Sept. 26, 1915; Hugh Pierson Bowden (526) killed in action Nov, 20, 1917; Edward Charles Bradbury (103); Wilfred Bradley (398) died of wounds Oct. 17, 1916; John Breen (67) killed in action July 1, 1916; Jonathan Brett (537); Patrick Brien (80); Edward John Brown (545) killed in action July 1, 1916; John Joseph Brown (537); Charles Burdell (330); Joseph Burn (527); William G.H. Burns (160); Hubert Frederick Burridge (191); Gladstone R. Burt (54); Harold Burt (323); Ernest Butcher (430); Alfred Francis Butler (460); Charles Oakley Butler (205); George Butler (457); Henry Albert Butler (325); Gerald Guy Byrne (340); Martin Joseph Cahill (258), killed in action July 1, 1916; John Caldwell (151); Roger John Callahan (344) killed July 1, 1916; Arthur R. Canham (221); Maurice Carberry (382); William Patrick Carew (469); Thomas Colton Carmichael (126); Thomas Carroll (274) killed July 1, 1916; James Carter (269); James Henry Carter (222) killed Nov. 20, 1917; Llewellyn James Carter (198) died of wounds July 2, 1916; John Simon Cashin (233); John Joseph Caul (374); Eric R.A. Chafe (52); George Wilbur Chancey (78); John Cuthbert Channing (347); John Fielding Chaplin (584) died of illness January 1, 1915; Thomas Christopher (121); Ernest St. Claire Churchill (281); William Maxse Churchill (4); Lawrence Edward Clare (343) killed in action Oct. 12, 1916; Robert Clare (210);

William Joseph Clare (536); George S. Claridge (110); Selby Clark (239); George Clarke (271) died Nov. 24, 1915; John Cleary (288) killed in action July 1, 1916; John Sullivan Cleary (131); William Cleary (384); Cecil Bayly Clift (505), killed in action Oct. 12, 1916; John Clift (503); Frederick Augustus Clouter (422); Arthur Colbourne (444); Edward Louis Cole (195) killed in action Jujly 28, 1916; Samuel Cole (465) killed in action Oct. 9, 1917; George Colford (16); James Collins (567) killed in action April 14, 1917; John Collins (578); William Joseph Collins (82) died of sickness Oct. 28, 1915; James Patrick Connors (209) killed in action July 1, 1916; Thomas Joseph Connors (170); Peter Joseph Constantine (563); Henry William Cook (483) killed Oct. 12, 1916; William Cook (553) died of wounds April 26, 1918; Archibald Coombs (492); Harry Coombs (393) killed in action July 1, 1916; Herbert George Cooper (439); James Cooper (98); Eugene Cornect (429); Edwin Cornick (377); Nathaniel Crane (363) killed in action April 14, 1917; Stan F. Crotty (459); Hebert Cuff (529); Frederick Curran (122); Peter Daniels (318); Henry Charles Dawwe (589) killed in action July 1, 1916; Joseph Dawe (328); Wilfred Dawe (184); William Gordon Dawe (97); Joseph Daymond (607); Wilbert Albert Delaney (581); Daniel Alexander Desroches; Herbert Dewling (45); Stewart Dewling (20); Christopher Bertram Dicks (33); William Patrick Dohaney (496) killed in action July 1, 1916; John Joseph Dooley (474); John Dunn (172); John Dunphy (44)killed in action Dec. 12, 1915; William Dunphy (15) killed in action July 1, 1916; Bill Eaton (137); Hubert Edgar Ebsary (339) killed in action Dec. 1, 1915; Samuel Joseph Ebsary (501) killed in action Oct. 15, 1916; Charles LeGallais Edgar (199) killed in action Feb. 26, 1917; Edward Francis Edgecombe (40) killed in action Aug. 21, 1917; John Charles Edwards (450) died of wounds July 21, 1916; John Elliott (22) killed in action July 1, 1916; John Joseph Ellis (443) killed in action July 1, 1916; Joseph Erley (116); Joseph Wellington Evans (181) killed in action July 1, 1916; Stewart Small Ferguson (95) killed in action July 1, 1916; Samuel Fiander (467); Charles William Field (115); Larry Field (153); Isaac Fifield (420); Maxmillian William Fillier (507); John Fitzgerald (295) killed in action Dec. 1, 1915; Richard Francis Fleming (357); Bernard Forsey (12); James Francis Fowler (311); William Fowler (81) killed in action July 1, 1916; John Ed. Joseph Fox (142); Charles Sydney Frost (58); John Joseph French (63) killed in action July 1, 1916; Nicholas Augustus Galgay (338); John Gardner (144); Frederick Garf (125) killed in action July 1, 1916; Charles Frederick Garland (182); George Stanley Garland (200); William Thomas Gellately (100); Arthur Wilfred Gillam (454) killed in action July 1, 1916; Edward Francis Gladney (335) killed in action July 1, 1916; William Joseph Gladney (417); Malcolm Godden (615); Archibald Gooby (154); Robert Joseph Good (219); Josiah Robert Goodyear (573); Stanley Charles Goodyear (334) killed in action Dec. 28, 1917; Gilbert Thomas Gordon (64); Frank George Gough (132); William Hoyes Grant (410) killed in action July 16, 1916; Augustus Peter Green (251);John Henry Stanley Green (108) killed in action July 1, 1916; Gordon Green (156); Walter Martin Greene (266) killed in action Nov. 20, 1917; William Joseph Greene (320); Robert Cecil Grieve (13);Joseph Patrick Griffin (577); Philip John Grouchy (369); T. J. Hackett (408); Robert Hayley(489); William Hall (352) killed in action Oct. 14, 1918; Arthur Hammond (79); Charles Hammond (594); Thomas Hammond (360); James Patrick Haney (476) killed in action July 1, 1916; Jacob Hann (90); Herbert Harding (353) killed in action April 23, 1917; William Frank Hardy (179) killed in action Sept. 23, 1915; Walter Joseph Harnett (458); Lawrence George Harsant (431); Arthur Piercey Hartley (174); Leonard Vincent Hartley (294); Gerald Harvey (333); Wilfred Eric Harvey (324); George Bernard Hatfield (65) killed in action July 1, 1916; Herbert Stephen Heater (180); Robert Henderson (471); Alexander Hennebury (461); Edwin Hennebury (19); Hubert Clinton Herder (3) killed in action July 1, 1916; Ralph Barnes Herder (34); James Francis Hibbs (299); James Joseph Hickey (113); John Joseph Hickey (586); John Hickey (252); William Francis Hickey (119); John Hepditch (240); George Cranifod Hiscock (342); Edward John Hoare (453) died of sickness June 14, 1916; John Herbert Hockley (216) killed in action July 1, 1916; Aiden Joseph Hogan (237); Luke Holden (329) killed in action July 1, 1915; Patrick Hogan (555) died of wounds Jan. 29, 1916; Albert Norman Hooper (248); Thomas Anthony Horan (212); Lawrence Amour Hoskins (449); James Patrick Houlahan (500); James John Howard (560) killed in action July 1, 1916; Moses Howell (462); Thomas Humphrey (375); William Humphries (588); James Hunt (564); William Joseph Hurley (11); William Thomas Hussey (356) killed in action April 12, 1917; Harold Hutchings (602) killed in action July 1, 1916; William F. C. Hutchings (538); John Francis Hynes (238); James Main Irving (49); Arthur Joseph Jackman (533) killed in action April 14,1917; Cecil Stanley James (102); Charles Robert James (436); Thomas Lincoln James (370); Harold Clark Janes(109); Harold Wesley Janes (197); Thomas Patrick Janes (136); Walter Harold Janes (57); John Allan Jeans (424) killed in action July 1, 1916; Silas Jeffers (292) killed in action July 1. 1916; Jens William Jensen (569); Arthur Francis Jesseau (249); John Joseph Johnson (135) killed in action July 1, 1916; Edward Joy (502) died of sickness Oct. 14, 1918;Clifford H.O. Jupp (157) killed in action July 1, 1916; Leonard John Jupp (162); George Kane (208) killed in action Dec. 3, 1917; Joseph Arthur Kavanagh (106); Walter Kearley (552); William Wallace Kearney (68); Hubert John Keats (613); William Keats (203) killed in action April 14, 1917; Frederick Keel (490); Ernest Kelly (27); John Joseph Kelly (188); Michael Francis Kelly (148) killed in action July 1, 1916; Thomas Joseph Kelly (178) killed in action July 1, 1916; Leo Terrence Kennedy (224); Michael Francis Kennedy (355) killed in action July 1, 1916; William . Kenneth (127); Robert Kershaw (406) died of wounds March 9, 1918;

Stanley S. Kirby (242); George Samuel Knight (309) killed in action Dec. 2, 1915; Francis Herbert Knight (287); William Knight (373) killed in action July 1, 1915; William Blackler Knight (290) killed in action July 1, 1916; Ronald Stephen Lacey (77); Edward Lahey (259); Robert Joseph Lahey (254) killed in action July , 1916; James Lambert (387); George Langmead Junior (14) died of wounds Dec. 8, 1917; Cyril Larner (426); Edward Joseph Lawlor (477); Thomas Joseph Lawlor (535); Frederick Legrow (9); Frederick Pratt Legrow (404); Roy Bennett Leseman (220); Philip S. LeMessurier (62); David Lewis (96); John Lewis (189); Harold LIdstone (163) killed in action Nov. 20, 1917; Augustus Lilly (194) killed in action July 1, 1916; Frank Thomas Lind (541) killed in action July 1, 1916; Samuel Thomas Lodge (165) killed in action Oct. 1, 1915; William John Long (48); James Newton Loveys (359); George Lukins (544); killed in action July 1, 1916; John Lukins (547) killed in action June 28, 1916; John Luff (350); Isaiah McConnell (396); Patrick McDonald (230); John Patrick Macdonnell (582) died of sickness Oct. 29, 1915; James McGraw (104); Thomas Bernard McGraw (128); Andrew Joseph McKay (572) died of wounds July 12, 1916; John J. Mackey (278); Neil McLellan (50); Enest Frederick McLeod (24); Norman A. McLeod (158); Hector McNeil (31); Donald Fraser McNeill (411) died of wounds July 6, 1916; William Robert McNiven (279) killed in action July 1, 1916; Sylvester Madden (149); Henry Morton Maddick (140); Michael Maddigan (47); Michael J. Maddigan (183); Pierce Maher (591); James Thomas Mahon (114); Allan W. Mallan (413); Joseph Francis Maloney (385); Augustus Joseph Manning (177) killed in action June 1, 1916; Peter Mansfield (85); William Manston (327); Willis Manuel (272); Charles LLewellyn March (86); Alfred Marrs (105); Frederick Walter Marshall (608); Charles P. Martin (192); Eric S. Martin (616) killed in action July 1, 1916; Robert Berkley Martin (499); Ronald Martin (75); Harold Walter Matthews (358); Thomas Mouland (488); William May (351); Constantine Mayer (175); Allan Moyes (546) killed in action July 1, 1916; Frederick Courtney Mellor (91) killed in action July 1, 1916; Albert Mercer (264); Frederick Mercer (159); Albert Edward Metcalfe (256); James Mifflin (419); Victor William Miles (214) killed in action July 1, 1916; Benjamin Miller (300) killed in action Oct. 9, 1917; George Miller (587) killed in action July 1, 1916; William Miller (107) died of wounds Oct. 19. 1915; Joseph Milley (85); James William Moore (529); Harrison Moores (218); John Edgar Morris (120); Kenneth Morris (412) killed in action July 1, 1916; Michael William Morrissey (427); Thomas Patrick Morrissey (211); Edgar Page Motty (446); Abraham Thomas Mullett (437); Frank Mullins (525); Bernard Murphy (530); Edward Joseph Murphy (112) killed in action July 1, 1916; James Edward Murphy (401); Lawrence Murphy (196) killed in action July 1, 1916; Michael James Murphy (70); Walter L. Murphy (407) died of sickness Sept. 29, 1915; Alfred Seymour Murray (39); Matthew Joseph Miles (548); John Myrick

(99) killed in action Dec. 10, 1915; Edward Joseph Nauftall, died of wounds Sept 29, 1918; William John Neville (376) killed in action April 14, 1917; William Thomas Newell (520); Albert Stanley Newman (36); Archibald M. Newman (487) died of wounds July 3, 1916 John E.B. Nichol (129); John Nicholle (435); John Francis Nicho (336); Llewellyn Norman (425): William Leonard Norris (101); Frederick Thomas Noseworthy (527); Herman Noseworthy (354) killed in action July 1, 1916; Vincent Noseworthy (201); William Noseworthy (206) killed in action Oct. 9, 1917; Michael Nugent (428); Bertram William Oake (539); John Joseph Oakley (292); John Eugene O'Dea (455); Leo Patrick O'Dea (186); Albert O'Driscoll (551) killed in action July 1, 1916; Charles Cunningham Oke (60); Harris B. Oke (565); Patrick Joseph O'Keefe; William Joseph O'Keefe (521) killed in action July 1, 1916; James Joseph O'Leary (391) killed in action July 1, 1916; Joseph Olsen (313) killed in action April 14, 1917; Frederick Michael O'Neil (402); Martin Patrick O'Neil (468); Douglas McNeil Osmond (306) died of wounds July 8, 1916; Frank O'Toole (365)died of wounds Oct. 12, 1917;Alexander Edward Parsons (585); William John Parsons (585); Neil Patrick (51); Reginald Grant Patterson (504); George Paver (534); Chesley Morton Peet (235); Arthur Nicholas Penney (229); Robert Penney (559); Arthur Joseph Penny (6) missing, believed killed April 14, 1917; Thomas Avery Parsons (423);Walter James Petrie (566); Berkley Piercey (421) killed in action April 14, 1917; Walter Piggott (296); Ernest Pike (609); Richard Pittman (400) killed in action July 1, 1916; David Power (310); Arthur Milligan Pratt (522); Arthur Purchase (540); George Albert Raines (381); Hubert J. Randell (94); John Joseph Reardigan (72); George Wilfred Rees (388); Henry Reid (513); Robert Bruce Reid (593) killed in action July 1, 1916; Charles James Renouf (147); Arthur James Rendell (204) killed in action July 1, 1916; Leo T. Rendell (231); Finlay McK. Campbell Richards (8); William Walter Richards (41); Frank Richardson (66) killed in action Aug. 16, 1917; F.J. Ricketts (451); Pierce Rideout (228) died of wounds April 27, 1918; Frank Roberts (383) died of wounds Oct. 23, 1915; Frederick George Roberts (440); Walter Graham Roberts (368); Eric McKenzie Robertson (497); John Joseph Robinson (480); Charles Dalton Rogers (389);Edward Joseph Rogers (353) killed in action July 1, 1916; Thomas Edward Rogers (394) killed in action Oct.12, 1916: William Roost (76) killed in action March 2, 1917; William John Rose (217); Michael John Ross (250) killed in action July 1, 1916; Henry Mott Rowe (611) killed in action Nov. 20, 1917; Edward Clayton Rowsell (571) killed in action July 1, 1916; William Thomas Ryall (53) killed in action July 1, 1916; Bernard Ryan (123) killed in action April 14, 1917; John Joseph Ryan (38); Thomas Brown Ryan (260); William Joseph Ryan (133) killed in action July 1, 1916; Peter Samson (267); Michael Francis Sears (73); Horatius Seaward (172) killed in action Aug. 16, 1917; William Burton Shave (543); John Joseph Sheehan (35) died of sickness

Dec. 28, 1917; Richard John Sheppard (282); Robert C. Sheppard (473); George Shirran (493); Richard A. Shortall (395) killed in action July 1, 1916; William T. Simmonds (349) killed in action April 13, 1918; John Henry Simms (88); Robert Ronald Simms (576) killed in action July 1, 1916; Sydney Bemister Skeffington (59); Arthur John Skinner (202); Albert Ernest Slade (273); Harvey Haynes Small (302); William A. Small (614); Robert Templeton Smith (366); Roy Archibald Smith (379); Walter Smith (478); Michael Frank Smyth (512); Thomas Joseph Smyth (523); Frank Snelgrove (405); Hardy Frederick Snow (322) killed in action Oct. 12, 1916: James Snow (433); Joseph Henry Snow (474); William James Somerton (263); George Sparkes (253)) killed in action July 1, 1916; John Spooner (498); Herbert Spry (275); Charles Patrick Spurrell (378); Josiah Squibb (243) killed in action Oct. 19, 1915; Jack Squires (367); Anthony James Stacey (466); Owen William Steele (326) died of wounds July 8, 1916; Wilfed Down Stenlake (415); John Sydney Stevenson (32) killed in action April 14, 1917; Leonard Tretheway Stick (1); Robin Stick (46); Henry Skinner Stone (361); Llewellyn Stone (26); Harry Groves Strathie (494) killed in action July 1, 1916; Charles St. Clair Strong (30) died of wounds April 13, 1918; Augustus Leo Summers (93); Charles F, Taylor (293) killed in action July 1, 1916; George Hayward Taylor (28) killed in action July 1, 1916; Herbert Taylor (7); Victor S. Taylor (111); Walter Cameron Taylor (452); John Vincent Temple (232); Robert Tetford (277);Walter Leslie Thistle (215); James Elliott Thompson (61) killed in action March 3, 1917; John Thompson (139); Walter Thompson (138); Henry Tilley (307) killed in action April 14, 1917; Richard Tilley (21); Austin Gerald Tipple (583); James John Tobin (69) killed in action Nov. 20, 1917; Harry Alexander Tompkinson)298); William Trebble (18); George Beverley Tuff (2); James Roy Tuff (23) died of wounds April 28, 1917; Ralph Wellon Tulk (234); Stanley Gordon Tulk (268); Michaael Vail (155); Francis J. Vaughan (481) died May 22, 1918; Oscar Augustus Vaughan (337) died July 4, 1917; Richad H. Voisey (152);Frank Walsh (161); George Edward Walsh (506); Michael Francis Walsh (399) killed in action July 1, 1916; Patrick Joseph Walsh (286); Frederick Walter Waterman (441); Francis Emilie Watts (71); James Pittman Watts (397) killed in action Oct. 12, 1916; Rupert King Watts (276) died Sept. 27, 1915; Arthur Webber (236); Alfred Wells (416); William Emeel West (25); Herbert Wheeler (475); John Joseph Whelan (169); Michael Thomas Whelan (432); Charles Edward White (171); Douglas White (37); Edward White (486); William White (345) killed in action July 1, 1916; John Williams (5); Roland Williams (10); Henry Kelso Wilson (305); George Joseph Winslow (317); Edgar Windsor (472) killed in action Oct. 9, 1917; Stanley Charles Windsor (301); Ernest Wood (20); Frank Woodford (364) killed in action July 1, 1916; Edward Wyatt (371); Thomas Walter Wyatt (386); Gordon Bemister Yates (570); Andrew Yetman (43); William Yetman (610).

About the Author

Jean Edwards Stacey is a journalist in St. John's and author of Historic Homes of Newfoundland (DRC Publishing 1998). She is currently working on a number of books, including Historic Homes of Newfoundland and Labrador.

Newfoundland has always been home to Jean. She was born in her mother's hometown of Swansea, Wales, but grew up in Gander where her parents, Martin and Betty Edwards, still live. Her dad is from Lawn, Placentia Bay, and met her mother when he was stationed overseas with the 125th RAF (Newfoundland) Squadron during the Second World War.

Jean lives in St. John's with her husband, Peter Stacey.

Jean and Peter have three children: David, Robyn and Christopher.